A nostalgic look a

BIRMINGHAM TRAMS

1933-1953

Volume 2
The southern routes
Bristol Road routes, Cotteridge and the Moseley Road routes, plus Nechells and Bolton Road

David Harvey

Silver Link Publishing Ltd

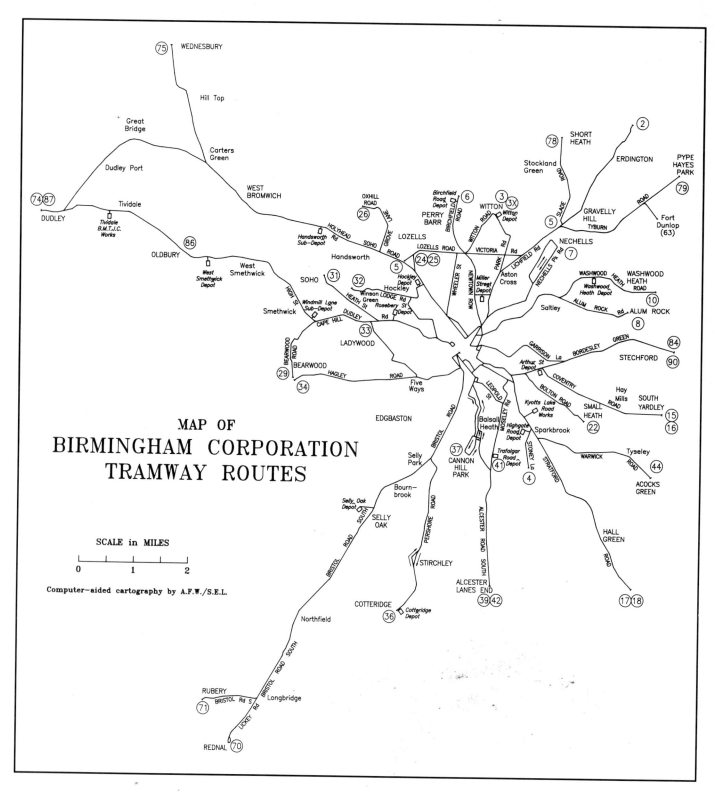

MAP OF
BIRMINGHAM CORPORATION
TRAMWAY ROUTES

SCALE in MILES

0   1   2

Computer–aided cartography by A.F.W./S.E.L.

Map of Birmingham Corporation tramway routes

This map shows the whole of the tramway network, including the northern routes featured in this book, but does not purport to show the system at any given date, being intended principally to locate each route to scale.

Only the route numbers of regular all-day tramcar services are shown.
For detail of trackwork and locations of short working turning points, see the definitive map by J. C. Gillham, extracts of which are given in each chapter.

ACKNOWLEDGEMENTS

THIS second volume of *A Nostalgic Look at Birmingham Trams* would not have been possible had it not been for all those tram enthusiasts and photographers whose work is credited within the main text.

I am extremely grateful to R. Brook, W. A. Camwell, John Edgington, F. N. Lloyd Jones, L. W. Perkins, K. Terry, C. C. Thornburn, J. S. Webb, Ray Wilson, and W. J. Wyse for allowing me access to their photographic collections and providing me with information and dates about their photographs. Special thanks must be given again to Geoffrey Morant for his invaluable work in helping me to find colour photographs of Birmingham's tramcars.

The contribution of Peter Jaques towards this volume, however, has been invaluable. But for his helpful comments and provision of factual data, this volume would have been considerably the poorer, and without his prompting much of the fascinating factual information about the history of the system and its rolling-stock would have been either missing or inaccurate. I would also like to thank his wife, Dorothy, for the many cups of coffee that she provided during our editing sessions.

I am extremely grateful to John Stanford for all his valuable comments about dates, advertisements and individual tramcar details, and to Richard Weaver for commenting upon and editing the manuscript. To Norman Glover, whose photographs appear in this volume, I extend special thanks as his personal recollections of Birmingham trams provide a fascinating insight into the system of over 40 years ago; he also took great care over the editing of the final draft of the text.

My thanks also go to John Gillham for allowing me to use extracts from his Birmingham track layout maps, to Stan Letts and Arthur Whitehouse for producing the general layout map of the Birmingham tram system and to Tony Hayward, who drove 2489, our preserved Birmingham Crossley double-decker bus, for my photographic reconstructions.

Finally, as before, I must thank my wife, Diana; her typing skills, critical comments, encouragement and patience made this second volume's production considerably easier.

First published in June 1994

British Library Cataloguing in Publication Data

A catalogue record for this book is available from the British Library

ISBN 1 85794 021 0

Silver Link Publishing Ltd
Unit 5
Home Farm Close
Church Street
Wadenhoe
Peterborough PE8 5TE
Tel/fax 0832 720440

Printed and bound in Great Britain

FOREWORD

Tony Britton

WE LEFT Birmingham in 1936, when I was 12. A long time ago. My memories of Birmingham and of the network of trams that carried Brummies to every corner of it are accordingly a little dim.

Playing them back on the mental television screen as I have been, to try to recall for you, dear reader, what the old city was like in those distant days, can be compared with watching an old, faded, badly edited black and white film with some scenes missing but lying around, somewhere, almost within reach.

It was when the Editor's letter arrived - 'Would I like to do a foreword about Birmingham trams?' - and I'd got over my surprise, that the first pictures began to flicker on the cerebral video: I was catching a tram, with my mother, near the council house. We were going to see my grandmother, who lived in a little house in a pattern of poor little streets off the Lichfield Road in Nechells. The pictures of the journey are fragmentary, but when we got off the tram and crossed the road and began to walk down Cuckoo Street (well, that's what my mother said it was called), there was the off licence on the corner, and there were the gas lamps (I can remember the gas lighter carrying his ladder from lamp post to lamp post), and the narrow alleys between the houses, and, suddenly, the interior of Grandma's own house.

Here I press the 'pause' button, and reflect that that huddled patchwork of terraced dwellings and the trams that used to take us there have vanished as though such things had never been, as has so much of the city of my childhood. Let's be grateful that it still lives on in the wonderful, evocative photographs and the nostalgic text that accompanies them in this volume and its predecessor.

Volume 1 has been a great stimulant to recollection. Browsing through it, the nostalgia promised in its title has been more than fulfilled by the memories revived - indeed, a wistful melancholy would be nearer the mark, as I turn the pages and see the trams travelling along old streets; passing hazily remembered shops and pubs; being overtaken by motor cars ('vintage', now - if you can find any!); vistas long-forgotten, with hoardings carrying posters for Beecham's Pills and Persil Whiteness and forgotten brands of cigarettes - ah! then you could buy five Woodbines in a paper packet for twopence. How friendly and kind and *innocent* those old ads seem now, light years away from the tastelessness and stridency of the advertising that scars our modern environs. Here are scenes of that far-off world preserved like flies in amber; one catches faint echoes of the rising growl of the tramcars' motors and the wheels grinding and jolting in the tracks.

Pressing the 'play' button and returning to my inner,

moving, pictures, here are more tram journeys, going to see uncles and aunts and cousins in Sutton Coldfield and Four Oaks (tram *and* Midland Red, perhaps?), and visiting my paternal grandfather in Gravelly Hill. He had a factory where the Britton bicycle pump was made - I had one on my first bike. Days out in Sutton Park, eating boiled eggs and bread and butter outside the café at Bracebridge Pool (I've never forgotten the flavour - much better in the open air). Fishing for tiddlers in Cannon Hill Park. Going to and from the Royal Mint Tavern in Icknield Street, of which more later.

The 'video' sequences become clearer. What unalloyed joy it was to leap on to the tram and rush upstairs to sit 'in front' on the outside deck, watching as the trolley pole was swung from end to end, a tricky business not always accomplished first time. The slamming noise as the slated seat-backs were reversed, the driver on his platform turning the knobbed lever and ringing his foot-operated bell and we were off, rattling and clanging and swaying, the breeze fresh in our faces.

There was a time, though, when the tram temporarily lost its enchantment and turned into a tumbrel, as it took me to school in Hagley Road to suffer bullying by older, bigger boys; a brief period I think, maybe only a few days, but long enough to make me play truant to get away from it. I would catch the tram as usual in the morning, but I would get off at Five Ways and take refuge in the little public garden there, with a book or a comic and, somehow, enough pennies to buy a Mars Bar and a Fry's Chocolate Cream to see me through the day until I reckoned school would be coming out and I could catch the tram back to home and safety. Inevitably my truancy, and the reason for it, were discovered and with encouragement from my father (no punishment, only understanding) I took on my chief tormentor one day and discovered that bullies are cowards. Life at school returned to normal and the tram, thank goodness, became once more a transport of delight instead of a boat across the Styx.

I mentioned the Royal Mint Tavern. I've been scouring Volume 1 for a tram passing that good old pub, on the 32 route, I think, but I can find only a mention in the text of the Royal Mint itself, which stood opposite the Tavern: 'At the bottom of the hill the cars passed the famous Birmingham Mint before crossing Icknield Street. . .' This is a great disappointment because my first memories of being alive were when we *lived* in the Royal Mint Tavern. My father managed it, and we lived over the shop, so to speak. After, we moved to the Trocadero in Temple Street, and a few years on, to the Market Hotel in Station Street, just behind New Street station.

During those years my mother, who loved the theatre

(as a girl she worked in the Box Office at the Aston Hippodrome), took me to see *everything* - music hall at The Empire, alas gone, and the Hippodrome, happily still with us. I saw great variety artists like George Robey, George Formby and Gracie Fields. At the Theatre Royal in New Street and the Prince of Wales in Broad Street, neither of which any longer exist, I saw great actors of the day, Owen Nares, Jack Buchanan, Cicely Courtneidge. Thanks to my mother, my childish mind must have absorbed a great deal that has been invaluable to me since.

Actors have childlike natures. Their work is so sophisticated and sometimes profound, but they must guard their ability to pretend, and to believe in princesses and dragons, as children do. They deal in dreams. They are by definition romantics.

What has all that to do with trams? Ah, but you see, there is drama and romance to this grown-up little boy in the hundreds of blue and primrose carriages that ferried us about the old city, while at the same time life was taking us all on *its* journey too, to meetings and partings, triumphs and disasters, love and loss of love, happiness and despair - the very stuff of romance!

In my travels in life, I've been reminded of route 32 in some unlikely places. The trams in Brussels in the war; the elderly and beautiful street cars of San Francisco roller-coasting gaily up and down the hilly city; and most sentimental of all, in Hong Kong, where there are lots of old British-style trams still patrolling the teeming streets, packing people in like sardines, prim and matronly and completely anachronistic, sedately threading their way between the magnificent towering glass and steel buildings of the city of the Taipans. A far cry from Brum and the 1930s.

I must press the stop button! I had no idea how many pictures lay in waiting, unseen for so long. . .

INTRODUCTION

THE Birmingham tram system was the fourth largest in Britain after London, Glasgow and Manchester, but to many tramway enthusiasts its tall, gaunt, dark blue and primrose tramcars all tended to look the same as each other. Yet, in a fleet totalling 843 cars owned by Birmingham Corporation, there were variations, modifications and differences among the 489 four-wheelers and the 354 eight-wheeled bogie tramcars. Although most depots had a selection of trams from a number of different types, there was a tendency for particular classes of tram to be associated with a group of routes at a specific point in time. The Cotteridge route was always linked to the 812 Class and the two lightweight trams, 842 and 843, while Moseley Road depot's 401 Class of open-balconied four-wheelers were rarely to be found anywhere else.

This second book continues the 'Nostalgic look at. . .' theme by showing the Second City's trams and their routes in a geographical, historical and social context. The streets of Birmingham that resounded to the rumblings of the trams have been largely altered out of all recognition. Redevelopment of the central area, either to replace time-expired buildings or to relieve congestion, swept away many landmarks such as Snow Hill Station, the subterranean toilets at the Dale End-Bull Street junction and the Kunzle's cake shop in Martineau Street.

In the inner suburbs, where the tramcar had reigned supreme as the transport for the 'working man', wartime bombing had cut great swathes through the Victorian terraces and the town planners were about to sweep away some 30,000 sub-standard back-to back properties. Housing in the city from the late 1930s was in a desperate plight; there were still 6,500 houses without a separate water supply, 81,500 without a bath and, as late as 1947, just over 400 properties without gas or electricity.

The inner areas of Ladywood, Newtown, Nechells, Highgate and Lee Bank were the first areas to be redeveloped and, in most cases, the passing of the tramcar was the prelude to a change in what had been a stable, if deteriorating, urban landscape; change that was to eradicate totally a way of life in the city. The mixture of houses and factories in areas such as Saltley, Duddeston and Aston disappeared, taking away whole communities from their dingy, treeless environments to the new estates being constructed either locally or at the edge of the city.

By the time that this redevelopment was starting, the trams had largely gone, and the more flexible bus was the prime mover of the population. When the trams finally were abandoned in the city, Birmingham had the dubious distinction of being the largest city in the world not to have any form of electric transport.

This book looks at basically the southern routes of the city, from about 1933, although earlier views are included. The routes covered in detail are the Bristol Road services, the Cotteridge route, the Moseley Road and Alcester Lanes End tram routes and the complex route network in the Balsall Heath area. As in the previous volume, each route is covered by a pictorial survey, using where possible previously unpublished photographs, from the city centre to the outer terminus. Two early abandonments are also covered in the volume; the first and second tram routes to be abandoned in the city were Nechells (1922) and Bolton Road (1930). These routes are not in the southern area of the city but are included here so that overall, in this series of books, the complete Birmingham system of tram routes, including those abandoned prior to 1933, can be covered. It is intended that the third volume will look at the western routes into the Black Country, the main eastern route to Stechford and the final abandonment of the Birmingham system in July 1953.

A BRIEF HISTORY OF
══ BIRMINGHAM CORPORATION ══
TRAMWAYS (1929-1945)

AT THE end of 1929 the Birmingham Corporation Tramways system was at its zenith. Two new lightweight tramcars, 842 and 843, had just been or were about to be delivered, and recent reserved track extensions to Hall Green and Stechford had been completed. The real situation, however, was that some of the 21 and 221 Classes of small four-wheelers were approaching the end of their lives and competition from bus services, which, of necessity, had to follow the main arterial routes out of the city, was starting to undermine the profitability of the trams on routes such as Hagley Road. The tram systems throughout the rest of the West Midlands were already beginning to wane. The last remnants of the once extensive BET-controlled companies in the Black Country were being closed in the Dudley area in 1929. Although BCT's trams 842 and 843 belonged to the start of Britain's second generation of tramcars, there was a hesitance by the Transport Department to have a long-term transport policy either for or against the trams despite the excellent fleet and track maintenance.

Following the model of the Nechells abandonment in 1922, the short and unprofitable Bolton Road route was abandoned on 5 February 1930 using one-man operated single-deck buses, as the track had become due for renewal. The Hagley Road 34 route had been in increasing difficulties for a number of years, as it was covered by other bus routes, and this largely unwanted service in the prestigious Edgbaston area was disposed of on 10 August 1930.

There was, however, plenty of opportunity for the tram system to expand as large housing developments were under way in areas such as Hall Green, Kingstanding, Shard End, Weoley Castle, Yardley Wood and Quinton. A few years earlier the tram had been instrumental in the opening up of such new suburbs, but other factors were now militating against it.

The late 'twenties had seen a great advance in the development of the motor-bus. By a curious irony, in November 1929, the same month in which Short Brothers-bodied lightweight tram 842 entered service, bus 338 (OF 3970), an AEC 'Regent' with a Brush body, entered service. For the first time a modern-looking bus, running on pneumatic tyres with an enclosed staircase and a powerful six-cylinder petrol engine, was to be seen on the streets of Birmingham. Gradually the tide was turning against the tram as this was the first of many Birmingham buses that were pleasant and sophisticated vehicles in which to ride.

The necessity to replace the original Railless trolleybuses of 1922 meant that after trying a number of demonstrators on loan, a fleet of new Leyland TB2s and AEC 663Ts was introduced on the Nechells route. The success of these trolleybuses was to have a major influence on the next conversion. Again, the need to replace the tracks along large sections of the Coventry Road tram route was the cause of the abandonment. The relative merits of the replacement mode of transport were considered at length. Despite the plethora of motor-buses that was demonstrated to the Transport Department between 1930 and 1933, the trolleybus won the day. On Sunday 7 January 1934 the new fleet of 50 Leyland TTBD2 six-wheeled trolleybuses started the replacement service to Yardley, and this was extended to the new housing estates in Sheldon on 5 July 1936.

This was electric power's last victory as Birmingham had found the answer to its public transport needs. The desire to support local industry had moved Birmingham away from the products of the London-based AEC. For bodies, there was little to rival Metro-Cammell's metal-framed products, but while all the demonstrators came and went, an order for some 50 double-deckers and 14 petrol-engined single-deckers was placed with Morris-Commercial of Adderley Park, Birmingham. They were not mechanically successful, but one of the Daimler demonstrators of 1932 had not only been fitted with a pre-selector gearbox, but also had a Gardner 5LW oil engine. In the space of 32 months Birmingham had in service exactly 400 of the new Daimler COG5 double-deckers, which were given fleet numbers from 564 to 963, and 55 similar single-deckers numbered 32-76. If the Transport Department had not officially decided on the abandonment of the system, then the arrival of these buses was instrumental in turning the future transport needs of the city away from the tramcar.

The Stratford Road group of routes was the next to go. Although trams served the two main arterial routes of Stratford Road to the Shirley boundary and Warwick Road as far as the Acocks Green shopping centre, the new council estates in Acocks Green, Hall Green and Warstock were served by buses. This led to unnecessarily large numbers of buses and trams competing for the same passengers on the trunk sections of the various bus routes. In the early hours of Wednesday 6 January 1937, totally enclosed bogie tramcar 564 was pulled by enthusiasts through the rain along the 200 yards from Stratford Road to Highgate Road depot and the following morning the lack of clatter from the trams made local residents aware of the comparative silence of the replacement Daimler buses.

Throughout the seven-year period from the delivery of the last two trams, there had been a rationalisation of the tramcar fleet. The old four-wheel trams of the 21 and 221 Classes, with the exception of the small bow-collector-fitted Brill-Maley cars that operated on the Lodge Road

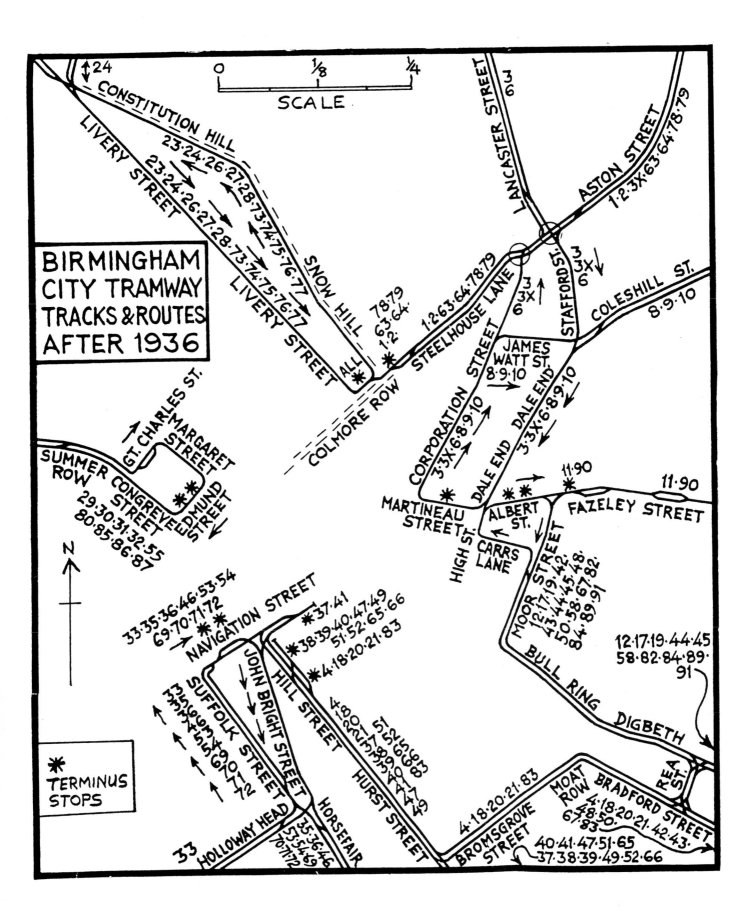

route, were gradually being withdrawn from the fleet. The closure of routes enabled the large fleet of bogie cars to be re-allocated, and after the Stratford Road closure a start was made on the scrapping of the open-balconied 71 Class Peckham-trucked tramcars.

There had in fact been a new section of track opened, when, on 13 February 1930, ex-CBT car 472 was decorated for the opening ceremony of the short Holly Lane branch off Tyburn Road to the Fort Dunlop factory. Another stretch of new track was opened on 25 September 1938 when the Erdington trams were diverted from the High Street and on to the reserved track in Sutton New Road. This was the final section of new tram route to be built in the city.

A measure of the change in policy was made apparent in November 1937 when the title of the undertaking was changed from the Birmingham Corporation Tramway & Omnibus Department to Birmingham City Transport. However, the next abandonments were forced upon Birmingham Corporation by factors beyond its control. In May 1937 West Bromwich Corporation decided that it would not renew its agreement with Birmingham to operate its Dudley and Wednesbury services, despite the extensive renewal of the track beyond Carters Green in 1933 and the use of high-powered bogie trams. West Bromwich wanted to use trolleybuses on the joint service, but, perhaps surprisingly, with the success of the Coventry Road trolleybus routes, Birmingham would not agree and decided reluctantly to close the whole section, despite the initial proposition to retain all the routes within the city. On Saturday 1 April 1939, after a four-month delay to allow for the delivery of new buses and the enlargement of Hockley depot, another of the Brush-built 512 Class, car 551, the last tram to leave Wednesbury, transferred its passengers at Carters Green to four-wheeler 128, which was due to be scrapped, and this tram took those people to Whitmore Street, Hockley.

The second abandonment of 1939 was caused by the termination of the Dudley Lease on the last day of 1938 and the purchase of the remaining company sections by the local authorities of Oldbury, Rowley Regis, Smethwick and Tipton. The Corporation continued to operate the trams on 'The Track' to Smethwick, Oldbury and Dudley on behalf of the various local authorities. It was decided to stop the tram service on 30 September 1939; the state of the track, especially beyond Smethwick, was very bad, and the route was operated exclusively by the oldest four-wheelers in the fleet from the 71 Class. Despite the declaration of the Second World War on 3 September 1939 and the operating and fuel restrictions that came into force almost immediately, it was decided to proceed with the abandonment which took place as planned.

Plans had been provisionally made to include the Lodge Road and Ladywood routes with the Dudley via Smethwick abandonment, but these were shelved because of the outbreak of war. Also the proposed abandonment of the Stechford routes, intended for April 1940 to coincide with the start of building of a dual carriageway in Digbeth and Deritend, was held back. This would have eliminated most of the 301 Class of four-wheelers from the fleet, but of course the need to save precious fuel meant that the trams had to soldier on.

The wartime bombing of Birmingham wreaked havoc with the tram services, particularly in the period from October 1940 to April 1941. No fewer than 43 trams were damaged beyond repair on raids on Witton, Washwood Heath and, worst of all, Miller Street depots. On 10 April 1941, after the worst air-raid on the city, no tramcar could reach its city terminus. After this things slowly returned to at least some pattern of normality. Some trams due for overhaul had to be repainted in an all-over grey livery and service cuts continued throughout the war, but there were no further tramway closures. The Nechells trolleybus route, however, had been closed on 30 September 1940 because the pyrotechnic display from the skate which had to be towed behind the trolleybuses in the tram track when they travelled between Washwood Heath depot and Bloomsbury Street was unacceptable in blackout conditions.

With the return to peace in 1945, it quickly became apparent that the trams would be withdrawn as soon as post-war deliveries of new buses could be obtained.

To be concluded in Volume 3

Right An unidentified, open-vestibuled, four-wheel Radial tram, of the 71-220 Class, climbs Nechells Park Road near Stanley Road, on the inward leg of its loop around Nechells. This car's fleet number cannot be identified clearly but it has only two digits and is therefore numbered in the 80 or 90 series. It is carrying the pre-1915 flop-over destination boards at the front of the open balcony. Just below it, on the dash panel, the tram is advertising the Empire Theatre, which was on the corner of Smallbrook Street and Hurst Street. The CBT horse tram service had its city terminus in Albert Street and was the last horse tram service to operate in Birmingham. It used ten specially constructed knife-board double-deckers which were kept in a depot off Nechells Park Road in nearby Butlin Street.

The boy with the hoop stands at the corner of Chattaway Street in front of the steeply descending terraced housing, of a slightly superior nature with wrought-iron fencing and their small downstairs bay-windows. With the young lady dressed in the shorter skirt and the older woman in the more conservatively styled long skirt, this view dates from about 1910.

The route was finally abandoned on 26 November 1922, and without ceremony trolleybuses took over, although they did not use the outer one-way leg along the parallel Long Acre. *Commercial postcard*

EARLY ABANDONMENTS

Nechells

THE Nechells route was opened on 1 January 1907 to replace the last CBT horse tram route in the city. This had its terminus at the bottom of Albert Street and had gone via Curzon Street, Vauxhall Road and Bloomsbury Street before gaining the steep descent past the stables and depot in Long Acre.

The replacement electric tram service, which in 1915 was numbered 7, had its city terminus at the top of Martineau Street, and was usually operated by four-wheel Radial cars from Washwood Heath depot. The route followed the Perry Barr trams along Corporation Street, but then went into Aston Street as far as Gosta Green. The trams left this former medieval open space and passed into Lister Street, crossing Holt Street, with its brewery, before launching themselves over the humped-back bridge that carried Lister Street over the Birmingham & Fazeley Canal and on towards the distant Nechells gas works. At the bottom of the bridge was the important factory-lined Dartmouth Street, and beyond the mixture of houses and small workshops that lined Great Lister Street. The route continued towards Saltley for about half a mile until it arrived at Bloomsbury Street, just before Saltley Road, where it would have met the Washwood Heath and Alum Rock tram routes. It then turned left into

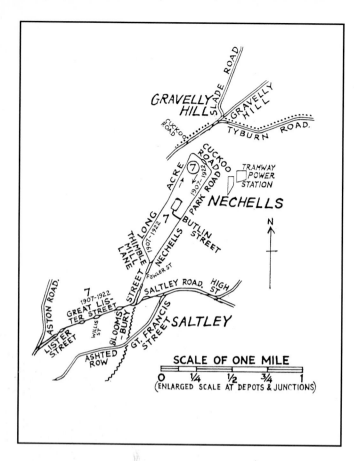

Nechells route

Bolton Road

THIS service was one of the many that were opened on 1 January 1907 as part of the enormous expansion of the tramway network embarked upon by Birmingham Corporation Tramways Department.

Starting in Station Street, the Bolton Road service followed the route of Yardley trams out of the city by way of Dudley Street, Pershore Street, Moat Row, Bradford Street and Rea Street, before gaining Digbeth and High Street, Deritend. The urban landscape was that of markets, warehouses and shops, which gave way to the residential areas of Bolton and Byron Roads.

The tram route turned left into Coventry Road and under the Great Western Railway's bridge at Bordesley. A little under 50 yards later the route crossed the Birmingham & Warwick Canal, and before the climb of Kingston Hill, towards Arthur Street depot, could be started, the route turned right into Bordesley Park Road. From here to the terminus, some one and a half miles away, the route ran to the north side of the extensive GWR sidings that lay alongside that railway's main line to London.

The trams ran through an area of late Victorian terraces, those in Bolton Road being earlier than those in Byron

Bloomsbury Street, regaining the former horse tram route.

The route climbed gently to the north-east until Nechells Green was reached at the corner of Nechells Place. From here the route began to run on a clockwise one-and-a-half-mile loop around Thimble Mill Lane and Long Acre to Cuckoo Road where the terminus was situated, then back up Nechells Park Road's hill and through the area's principal shopping centre before returning to Nechells Green.

The area had been developed in the 1840s with back-to-back houses mixed in with the later bye-laws terraces of the 1860s and 1870s. Some slightly more prosperous houses had been built at the northern end of Nechells Park Road, but the area around Cuckoo Road, sandwiched between Tame valley, with its sewage filter beds to the north, the Birmingham & Fazeley Canal with its associated industrial development to the west, and to the east the dismal mass of Nechells power station, was not really conducive to attracting wealthy Victorians.

With the Chairman of the Tramways Committee, Alderman Harrison Barrow, keen to implement trailer operation using single-deck tramcars, the Nechells route was selected in 1916 to try out this experiment, as it had loop termini at both inner and outer ends. The experiment ended in 1918 and the route, in urgent need of new track but poorly subscribed, was finally abandoned on 26 November 1922. It was replaced the next day, becoming the first tram route in the country to be converted to trolley-bus operation, using a batch of solid-tyred, Roe-bodied, top-covered Railless double-deckers.

Road, which was reached after the pastorally named Golden Hillock Road was crossed. The late-19th-century developers in this part of Small Heath evidently had a penchant for literature, as the trams turned right into Waverley Road opposite Tennyson Road. This junction was at the southern corner of Small Heath Park, the land for which had been donated by Miss L. A. Ryland and had been opened to the public in 1878. The park had been visited by Queen Victoria on 23 March 1887, the same day that she laid the foundation stone for the Victoria Law Courts in the town centre, and for a time the park was known as Victoria Park to commemorate the visit. The Coventry Road trams could be seen on the far side of the park as the route left its oasis and the large contemporary villas that skirted it and ran to the stub terminus in

Waverley Road at the junction with Oldknow Road in the shadow of the BSA factory.

Under the 1915 route numbering system the Bolton Road tram route was allocated number 22, and for most of its life it was operated by small four-wheel trams from the 21 and 71 Classes or ex-Company cars. The service was unremunerative because it relied only upon the BSA works traffic, the comparatively small amount of housing along the route with virtually no housing to the south side of Bolton Road, and its proximity to the Coventry Road services. It was the second tram route to close, and car 294 performed the final duties on Tuesday 4 February 1930. The service was replaced by one-man-operated Guy single-deck buses, and eventually the service became part of the circuitous 28 route on 2 October 1935.

Right UEC-bodied Brill 21E-trucked tram 46 is in its almost original condition in Byron Road near the junction with Golden Hillock Road in about 1908. These small 48-seater trams, bodied by the United Electric Car Co of Preston, of which there were 130 delivered to BCT between 1905 and 1908, were the backbone of the Edwardian tramcar fleet. Even if their three-windowed, open-topped, wooden-seated, unvestibuled condition seemed a little primitive, these little tramcars could go anywhere on the expanding tramway system.

By 1910 this car had been fitted with the Maley track brake, becoming one of 54 'Brill-Maley' cars. This particular tram was later fitted for snowplough operation along with 59 others of the class, and received top covers and vestibules. Having run from Coventry Road for most of its life, car 46 then moved to Rosebery Street and later Witton from where it was withdrawn in February 1937. *Commercial postcard*

Left The terminus of the 22 Bolton Road route was on the Oldknow Road corner just before the BSA works. At the twin terminal lines was a crossover used to gain access to the city-bound line.

Ex-CBT car 461 (formerly 201 in the CBT fleet) stands on the outbound stub, with the ubiquitous corner shop opposite the BSA factory. Known as the 'Aston' type, these trams were originally built by the Brush Company in 1904. By about 1929, when this photograph was taken, it had acquired a top cover and a vestibule. It is known to have been a Highgate Road tram in 1929, suggesting that this photograph was taken on a Sunday, for on this day Coventry Road and Highgate Road depots worked alternate journeys on the short Stoney Lane 4 and Bolton Road services from 1928 until the latter route's abandonment on Tuesday 4 February 1930. *R. T. Coxon collection*

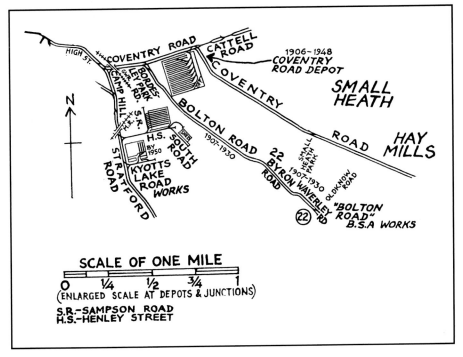

Right Coventry Road route

BRISTOL ROAD ROUTES

Bristol Road, Bournbrook, Selly Oak, Northfield, Longbridge, Rednal and Rubery

ON 24 July 1890 the Birmingham Central Tramways Co Ltd began a service along Bristol Road that was worked by accumulator cars. These looked very similar to the existing cable trams that were in operation on the Handsworth route. This unusual battery-powered method of transport used bogie cars 101-112, built by Falcon. Numerically they followed on from the 25 Handsworth cable cars. There were also two small four-wheeled accumulator cars built by Brown Marshall in 1893, but these only ran for a short time. The battery cars had replaced a 4 ft 8½ in standard gauge horse tram system operated by the Birmingham & District Tramways Company, which had operated to the Bournbrook boundary at the Bournbrook Hotel from 1873.

The new method of transport terminated at Dawlish Road, just beyond the horse-tram terminus, where a new depot was built to accommodate the cars. The accumulator tramcars had a 48-seat capacity, which enabled them to move large numbers of passengers, but problems with maintaining and recharging the batteries together with leakages of acid from them meant that this type of tram was not totally successful.

After the City of Birmingham Tramways Company was set up on 29 September 1896 to take over the assets of the Birmingham Central company, the decline in the reliability of the battery accumulator trams caused CBT to approach the Birmingham Corporation Public Works Department with a view to rebuilding the Bristol Road line using a new fleet of overhead electric tramcars. These were introduced on Tuesday 14 May 1901, and the opportunity was taken to extend the line almost another half a mile south-westwards to Chapel Lane, Selly Oak. This was the first overhead electric route to be opened in Birmingham and utilised 15 small 48-seater trams constructed by the ER&TCW, numbered 151-165.

When opened, the electric trams' city terminus was, like its predecessor, at a dead-end terminus in Suffolk Street. This terminus was considered to be too far away from the city centre, and on 4 February 1902 an anti-

clockwise loop was brought into use. This used an inward line from the Horse Fair along John Bright Street to a terminus at the west end of Navigation Street near to New Street Station. It then turned left into Suffolk Street and back to the Horse Fair. It will be noticed that this is the reverse of the way that the loop is shown in Birmingham Corporation days, and was only changed to the more usually seen clockwise route when the Ladywood electric tram service was introduced on 17 October 1906. After this date the route itself remained largely unaltered until 1923, when the outer terminus was placed on the south side of Chapel Lane.

On leaving the terminus in Navigation Street over the western tunnel leading into New Street Station, the trams turned left into the busy built-up office area in John Bright Street. This road had been opened in 1881 and had swept away some of the worst slums in Birmingham in Cross Street and Gough Street; it opened up the town to the south-west and by the early years of the century had the added attraction of the Alexandra Theatre, which was opened in May 1901 and was originally known as the Lyceum.

After passing Station Street, which had been used by the steam trams until the end of 1906, the important junction with Suffolk Street, Holloway Head and Smallbrook Street was reached. The trams headed southwards across this junction and passed into the Horse Fair. The tram route had by now left the late Victorian redevelopments of the city and passed into the much older houses that lined the Horse Fair. This wide road was made available for the trading of horses in the late 18th century and became a prosperous market area. At Essex Street, the road turned to the south-west into Bristol Street. This street became important during the time of the horse-trams, which were introduced in the 1870s, and it prospered as the shopping area for the people of the Edgbaston and Balsall Heath suburbs around the St Lukes Road junction.

At the end of the shopping suburb at Belgrave Road, Bristol Road climbed sharply until Wellington Road was reached. From here until Priory Road and Pebble Mill Road, the route skirted the end of the Calthorpe Estate, which lay to the west. This straight section of Bristol Road was developed, from the late Regency period, as a high-class residential area with substantial houses in large grounds for the dignitaries and industrialists of Birmingham. Priory Road connected the affluent suburbs of Edgbaston and Moseley and crossed Bristol Road at the southern end of its Victorian residential growth. Just beyond this was the junction with Pebble Mill Road, where the Cotteridge-bound trams turned towards Pershore Road.

After 1924 this section of the Bristol Road route was re-positioned on to a central reservation. The last 600 yards of this section of reserved track from Eastern Road to Edgbaston Park Road was developed with bay-windowed inter-war houses on the south-eastern side and opposite, beyond the playing fields, the school buildings of the King Edward foundation. It was along this tree-lined avenue that, after the trams were abandoned on 5 July 1952, some of the withdrawn tramcars were stored for up to three weeks before being driven away to Witton depot for scrapping.

On the hill behind the Gun Barrels public house, on the corner of Edgbaston Park Road, stand the buildings of the University of Birmingham; these were begun in 1900 and opened with much civic ceremony by King Edward VII in July 1909. The University, which is actually in Edgbaston, is dominated by the Great Hall and the campanile (bell tower), both of which could be seen from a passing tramcar, some 300 yards away. The Gun Barrels public house stood virtually on the county boundary with Worcestershire and had been a centre for bare-knuckle prize fighting.

After crossing the Bourn Brook stream, the trams entered the Victorian development of Bournbrook. The route went through an area that has survived virtually intact today as a suburban shopping centre. The old

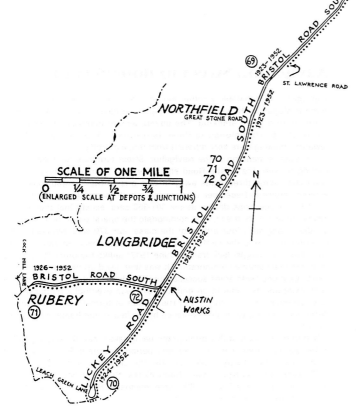

Bristol Road routes

horse tram stables behind the Bournbrook Hotel, renamed in the 1980s as The Old Varsity Tavern, were on the west side of Bristol Road, in Grange Road. Opposite, between Dawlish Road and Tiverton Road and still standing, was the former CBT Bournbrook accumulator and subsequent electric tramcar depot. Bournbrook depot had been built in 1891 and was to serve the Corporation's trams from its takeover of the operation of the Bristol Road routes on 1 July 1911 until the overcrowded depot was replaced by the new premises at Selly Oak.

Bristol Road then climbed a long steep incline, passing the Selly Oak Institute, built with money given by George Cadbury in 1894, before passing beneath the bridge that carried the former Midland Railway's Birmingham and West Suburban line. This line, with its later re-aligned bridge and track, and Selly Oak station just beyond the bridge on the south side of Bristol Road, had been opened initially on 3 April 1876 between the dead-end terminus at Granville Street and the Camp Hill line at Kings Norton, and had provided competition with the trams as a major carrier of commuter passengers along the Bristol Road corridor. Once the Worcester & Birmingham canal, alongside which the Midland Railway constructed its line, was crossed, the tram route reached the top of the hill and arrived at Selly Oak, which was the third shopping area on the route. This original part of the service was numbered 35 after 1915 when route numbers were introduced.

The terminus at the Plough & Harrow public house, on the corner of Chapel Lane, also marked the position of the branch line to Selly Oak depot. This was opened with a capacity of some 80 tramcars on 12 July 1927. After 1 October 1923 the tram route was extended from Selly Oak, along further stretches of reserved track to Northfield, which was some two and a half miles away. On leaving the shopping centre at the southern end of Selly Oak, the trams crested the top of Griffins Hill at Weoley Park Road and descended the steep hill, passing the Methodist Teacher's Colleges before reaching the wooded valley bottom at Bournville Lane and the small bridge over Griffins Brook. This area is still largely protected from urban growth as the land is owned by the Bournville Village Trust.

A further climb along the tree-lined central reservation took the tram service past the Orthopaedic Hospital and into the fourth suburban shopping centre on the route, which was the 69 route terminus. This service was developed to serve the commuter suburb that had grown as a result of the opening by the Midland Railway of its railway station at Northfield in 1869. The later Edwardian growth to the east of the main Bristol Road had gradually spread away from the medieval village centre and the need for a cheap, alternative method of transport was met by the Corporation tramcars. It was a vicious circle, as the introduction of the trams led to further urban expansion, so that the almost rural nature of the Bristol Road in the Northfield of the 1920s was soon to be eclipsed by expansion and left behind by a further tramway extension.

On 17 December 1923 the service was extended as the 72 route to Longbridge to replace the connecting bus services between Northfield and Longbridge, Rednal and Rubery. This extension had first been worked on 19 July 1913 using ten Daimler 40 hp motor-buses. These were the first motor-bus-operated services run by Birmingham Corporation and continued, despite the trials and tribulations of the First World War, until being eventually replaced by the tramway. The Austin Motor Works had been opened in 1905 near to the junction of the Halesowen branch line on the Midland Railway's main line between Birmingham and Gloucester. After the ending of hostilities, the ribbon development of mainly bay-windowed semi-detached houses spread rapidly southwards away from Northfield down the steep Pigeon House Hill and subsumed the areas around the old cluster of houses at Tessall near the Austin factory. As with the Selly Oak to Northfield section, this stretch of track was laid on central reservation.

The route was next extended to Rednal on 14 April 1924, alongside Cofton park to the Hare and Hounds public house up the increasingly steep climb of Lickey Road. Although served for the previous 11 years by buses, the new 70 route enabled passengers to travel far more easily from the city terminus at Navigation Street the eight and a quarter miles to the open spaces of the Lickey Hills; this enabled the terminus area to be developed as a local tourist attraction. The following year, the distinctive

200-yard-long terminal loop with its large curved wrought-iron shelter was constructed. Originally the tramway along Lickey Road was built on the western side of the road, and when the second carriageway was built in 1939 this became the central reservation.

The last part of the Bristol Road group of routes to open was westwards along Bristol Road South to the gates of Rubery Hill Hospital near Cock Hill Lane. The 71 route served the Leach Green housing development that nestled beneath the 821-foot Rednal Hill to the south of the extension. This one-mile section on reserved track was opened on Monday 8 February 1926 but, unlike the 1913 open-topped bus service, did not cross the city boundary into Rubery.

The Bristol Road route was for many years operated largely by the 301 Class of open-balconied four-wheelers, which saw sterling service and operated on the route until 1939. After this date they were superseded by bogie-cars displaced by the closure of the Hockley services. Many of the 301 Class went to other depots to displace the ex-Radial 71 Class cars which were being withdrawn from the fleet. Towards the end of operation on the routes, more air-brake cars from initially the 732 Class and, after the closure of the Washwood Heath routes, the former bow-collector-fitted 762 Class were synonymous with this most impressive south-western section of Birmingham's tramway system, where the running time for a return trip was timetabled to take only 86 minutes.

The Bristol Road routes closed on Saturday 5 July 1952.

Navigation Street to Bournbrook

Top right It is debatable whether modern-day health experts would agree with the slogan for K4 cigarettes, but in pre-war days every film star looked more alluring when smoking. The advertisement displayed between the decks of car 379 belongs to those far-off days when social attitudes towards smoking were very different from those of today.

The tram is standing at the Navigation Street terminus on 7 April 1939, waiting to work the Bristol Road short-working, numbered Service 35, to Selly Oak, some three miles away. It was one of the 361-400 Class that entered service in December 1911, and was built by the United Electric Car Co (UEC) to the same design as the 301-360 cars, except that they were 6 inches longer, at 29 ft 9 in, to accommodate the operation of the handbrake handle. Along with four others of the class, car 379 was involved in the experiments during the First World War with single-deck operation, being converted to a single-deck tram in June 1917; unlike the other four, it was modified to a standee configuration. It was then used on the Cannon Hill 37 route, apparently with some success, but towards the end of 1918 the single-deck experiments came to an end. Car 379 was eventually refitted with a new top-deck cover in July 1923. The quintet of former converted single-deckers could always be distinguished by the lack of top-lights in the upper saloon.

Within three years of this photograph being taken, car 379 was repainted in the wartime grey livery after another period in store in Rosebery Street depot. It was eventually broken up after the closure of the Witton routes in February 1950 at Kyotts Lake Road Works. Standing behind the open-balconied tram is car 748, a 1926 totally enclosed, Brush-built tram, working the 70 route to Rednal. *L. W. Perkins*

Middle right The distant Victorian buildings of Stephenson Street and the edge of the central shopping area of the city are reminders that in Birmingham many buildings have outlived the tram, which occupied only a short phase of the recent history and growth of the city. Indeed, in view of the large-scale redevelopment that has taken place in the city centre, it is a little surprising that a number of existing city centre buildings actually pre-date the Bristol Road trams. The Bristol Road overhead electric trams ran from 14 May 1901 until 30 June 1911 in City of Birmingham Tramways (CBT) ownership; from the following day until the abandonment on 5 July 1952 the route was operated by Birmingham Corporation.

Tram 739, one of the first batch of air-brake cars purchased by the Corporation, was built by Brush Electrical Engineering and is seen here turning into the terminal kerb-side track in Navigation Street to pick up passengers for the long run, partly on reserved track, back to Rednal on the 70 route. This 60-seater car will join the later Short Brothers-built car 818 at the rather splendid cast iron shelters. Car 818 is working the 36 route to Cotteridge, and just behind it is one of the 20 Guy Arab IIIs owned by Midland Red, fitted with powerful Meadows engines and Guy-built bodies to Park Royal design. It is working on one of the routes to Dudley or Wolverhampton. There are only six cars and one van visible in this 1951 view of Navigation Street, including the early post-war, Warwickshire-registered Standard 8 in the foreground. *R. T. Wilson*

Bottom right The scene in Navigation Street in August 1993 is still recognisable as many of the distant buildings and the road layout remain the same as in tramway days. The splendid shelters that dominated the Hill Street end of Navigation Street disappeared within a few years of the end of the trams, while the large New Street Station signal box, with its rather dated concertina-shaped concrete sides, was brought into use on 3 July 1966. The traffic flow has changed in the intervening years and is back to being two way again. Just visible on the extreme right is New Street Station and the associated Birmingham Shopping Centre, now known as the Palisades, which reduced the run-down Victorian station to a far more dismal 1960s subterranean apology for a main-line station.

In the centre of the view are the late-19th-century buildings of Stephenson Street and Pinfold Street. These fortunately survived the 1960s wish to demolish any buildings that looked old, and have since been refurbished. The advertisement for Wills's Capstan cigarettes that dominated these buildings in 1951 has, however, long since gone; dominating the skyline today is the former Woolworth building, which was built on the site of the famous Theatre Royal. This old theatre was demolished in 1957 after the production of 'The Fol-de-Rols' closed on 15 December 1956. The replacement structure was in turn rebuilt in the late 1980s after F. W. Woolworth closed its former store.

The two buses, 1950 ex-Birmingham Crossley 2489 (JOJ 489) and MCW 'Metrobus' MK II 2690 (A690 UOE), represent the passenger transport scene from the late tramway period until the end of the 1960s and the modern bus scene in **Birmingham**. *D. R. Harvey*

Below The Bristol Road and Cotteridge cars on their inward journey from Horsefair travelled along Suffolk Street and descended to where they turned right into Navigation Street, where the terminus was situated. They then turned right again into John Bright Street before leaving this two-thirds of a mile triangle and rejoining Horsefair. One of the former Washwood Heath bow-collector cars, 768, a 1928 Brush car fitted with EMB air brakes and EMB-built Burnley-type maximum traction bogies, stands in Suffolk Street at the yellow tram stop in June 1952. A solitary passenger is caught alighting before the tram slowly turns into Navigation Street. This corner was the site of an unfortunate accident in 1942 when tram 587 over-turned after the driver accelerated down the short descent in Suffolk Street and failed to negotiate the sharp corner into Navigation Street after losing his bearings in the early morning blackout. The small boy on the pavement looks curiously over his shoulder at Ray Wilson, who took so many interesting photographs of the Birmingham transport scene in the early post-war period.

The only building to survive today is the distant Baskerville House at the top of Suffolk Street. This is the building to the left of the gap in the skyline and was the only wing completed of the neo-classical civic centre, in 1939. It was, according to its architect T. Cecil Howitt, based on the Belvedere Palace in Rome, but perhaps belongs better in the capital of a former communist country, as in certain quarters it is nicknamed 'The Kremlin'. Everything else has gone.

On the left of Suffolk Street is the West End cinema, opened on 9 March 1925 with a performance of *Zeebrugge*. and closed on 18 March 1967 to make way for the inner ring road scheme. The building standing on the corner of Holliday Street was the offices of the goods department of the former LMS Railway. This also disappeared, along with the buildings both opposite and behind the tram, with the construction of Suffolk Street Queensway and its tunnel, which starts approximately where the lone motor cyclist is riding. *R. T. Wilson*

Above Most views of Navigation Street looking away from the city centre towards Suffolk Street show lines of trams waiting to pick up passengers at the shelters before going off on their journeys to Cotteridge, Rednal or Rubery, although in earlier years trams for Ladywood also boarded here. It is therefore interesting to find a view of a Permanent Way car running in the city centre. These single-deck trams were usually old tramcars, which, when withdrawn, were fitted with two carborundum stones used to eradicate corrugations in the track by scrubbing the rail surface. Fixed to each side of the centre of the truck frame, these stones could be lowered on to the rails by means of rods and levers operated by a wheel. The PW cars had in their saloons four large water tanks to lubricate the operation.

PW9 was formerly ex-CBT 166 and was built as an open-top, open-vestibule, double-decker in 1903 by ER&TCW (Electric Railway & Tramway Carriage Works). It became car number 509 when acquired by the Corporation in July 1911, then in October 1916 was rebuilt as a single-deck non-powered trailer, initially behind car 431 on the Nechells route and from March 1917 until 1918 behind ex-CBT bogie car 451 on the Washwood Heath route. It then lay unused until December 1928 when it became PW9.

This 1951 view shows it running in full fleet livery on the outer line in Navigation Street, which bypassed the loading loop at the shelters. Behind the single-decker is the old Birmingham Technical School, which was opened in December 1895 and later became Central Grammar School. This terracotta-faced building was in nearby Suffolk Street, and dominated the skyline at that end of Navigation Street throughout the tramway era until it became a victim of the Suffolk Street Queensway inner ring road scheme in the late 1960s. A further sign of the post-war changes in the transport scene at this time is the distant bus, a 1950 Daimler CVD6 of the 2031-2130 Class working the replacement 48 route through Balsall Heath to the Maypole terminus beyond Kings Heath. *F. N. Lloyd Jones*

Left Further up Suffolk Street, car 522 climbs the rise from the end of Station Street in company with a 1949 Vauxhall Wyvern and in front of a splendid 1936 Austin Eighteen. From this vantage point Suffolk Street looked fairly flat, yet the road dropped quite sharply before rising to the distant buildings of the civic centre.

The tram is one of 75 cars built in 1913 with United Electric Car Co (UEC) bodies mounted on Mountain & Gibson Burnley maximum traction bogies and equipped with DK19A 40 hp Dick, Kerr motors. Originally fitted with open balconies, the class was totally enclosed between May 1926 and September 1931. Car 522 was one of ten of the class to receive a new top-cover in about 1929, which provided eight windows per side instead of the original four, to the same design as the contemporary 762-811 Class. It had been modified in 1927 by being fitted with GEC WT32R 70 hp motors, and in this form it was ideally suited to the fast running along Bristol Road's reserved track. Seen here in around 1949, still with the pre-war style of fleet number, car 522 is working the 71 route into the city from Rubery. It was not taken out of service until the final abandonment of the Bristol Road routes on 5 July 1952, along with all the other 70 hp cars, being broken up at Witton depot the same month. *F. N. Lloyd Jones*

Right The Bristol Road and Cotteridge trams turned sharp right into John Bright Street after leaving the Navigation Street shelters. Car 622, a 1920 Brush-bodied 60-seater, with Brush Burnley maximum traction bogies and DK30/1L 63 hp motors, negotiates this curve in June 1952. This all-electric tram was one of ten to travel across the city from Miller Street depot during these last two months of tramcar operation at Selly Oak depot. This was necessary as at least seven of Selly Oak's trams had been taken out of service prematurely, leaving the depot decidedly short of stock.

The body of 622 was considerably altered in its 33-year working life. Originally built with open balconies, it was totally enclosed in July 1928 when it received the revised layout of eight windows per side in the upper saloon. In 1948 it was one of nine of the 587-636 Class to have its body strengthened. This is evident in this view by the plated-over top-light windows at the extreme ends of the lower saloon. *R. Brook*

Middle right Another view of the turn from the terminus in Navigation Street into John Bright Street. Car 512, the first of the 75 bogie cars ordered in 1913, starts the short-working along Bristol Street to Selly Oak on the 35 route, and is about to cross the single-line junction that enabled Moseley Road cars, with their terminus in Hill Street and the railway station end of Navigation Street, to link with the trams coming from the Suffolk Street side of Navigation Street. This was also the track used by the Hagley Road and Ladywood trams as they started at the Queens Hotel end of Navigation Street, before crossing into John Bright Street and eventually reaching Hagley Road at Five Ways.

Car 512 was one of the 70 hp trams that had their bodies rebuilt in about 1948. This rebuilding could be easily identified because all the cars so treated had their platform bulkhead windows plated over.

This 1949 view was taken when the Hill Street bridge over the north-western end of New Street Station was being rebuilt. Daimler COG5 11187 (FOF 187) is glimpsed at the bottom of Hill Street and is crossing the temporary bridge above the railway lines. In those days Hill Street was considered a fearsome climb with a fully laden bus up under the bridge linking the two halves of the General Post Office, and into Victoria Square. The clock tower just visible is known as 'Big Brum'; it was designed by Yeoville Thomason in 1885 as part of the City Museum and Art Gallery building. Today the pedestrianised John Bright Street is a far cry from when it was one of the busiest city centre streets used by the trams. *F. N. Lloyd Jones*

Below left Car 516 travels away from Navigation Street past the bomb-damaged corner of John Bright Street at the junction with Hill Street on its way to Rednal. John Bright Street was named after a Victorian Member of Parliament; constructed in 1881, it opened up access to the south-west of the city centre, replacing the Inkleys Greens Village and Cross Street, in which were some of the most violent and notorious slums in Birmingham.

In the foreground is the track pointwork that connected the eastern end of Navigation Street to John Bright Street. This was used latterly for Selly Oak cars to gain access to Kyotts Lake Road works, but after the Moseley Road abandonments that depot's connection to the Bristol Road for the Lickey Hills extras was no longer required. A new cross-over direct from the western end of Navigation Street into Hill Street was constructed in April 1950.

This area of John Bright Street and Hill Street was very badly damaged on the night of 19/20 November 1940. A landmine destroyed the Malt Shovel public house on the island site between the two streets. By early 1950, when this view was taken, the site was still derelict, and it was to be more than another ten years before it was redeveloped. *D. Sanders collection*

Left The early post-war Riley Pathfinder has swept past car 741 in John Bright Street near the junction with Smallbrook Street. In the distance is the Horse Fair, and beyond that the main A38 Bristol Road to Selly Oak and Northfield. The stylish Riley, virtually the only car in sight, epitomised the last mass-produced cars to have streamlined wings and running boards.

Inbound trams went from the Horse Fair into Suffolk Street, which is to the right of this view. Most of the buildings behind the tram were demolished as part of the Smallbrook Ringway scheme begun in 1957. This was the first section of the Inner Ring Road to be completed and was opened on 11 March 1960 by the Rt Hon Ernest Marples MP.

Car 741 was a 63 hp tram. Entering service in November 1926, it belonged to the first class of cars, numbered 732-761, to be equipped with EMB Maley air-track and magnetic brakes. Originally allocated to Rosebery Street depot for the 33 route to Ladywood and the 34 route along the Hagley Road, it was transferred to Selly Oak in June 1934 and remained there until it was withdrawn in May 1952. *R. T. Wilson*

Below Although a major road, Smallbrook Street was only ever used for public transport by Midland Red buses. Car 808, one of the bow-collector cars recently transferred from Washwood Heath depot, leaves John Bright Street and, just beyond the bollard in the foreground, will meet the inbound line of the Bristol Road group of routes on their way to the Navigation Street terminus. Car 808 is seen in this 1951 view in the final post-war livery and carries on its side the famous 'Say CWS and Save' advertisement for the Co-operative group of shops. The tram was to see service until the closure of the Bristol Road group of routes on 5 July 1952 and was broken up at Witton depot later the same month. All the air-brake cars, despite having been built in 1926 and after, were broken up at this time as the drivers of the Aston Road group of routes worked the earlier, lower-horsepower all-electric-braked trams. It was considered inappropriate to retrain them on the newer air-brake cars for just one year's extra service. *C. Carter*

Top right The tram stop at the junction of Smallbrook Street (to the right) and Holloway Head (beyond the tall building to the left) in Horsefair was located in the middle of this important thoroughfare. Car 543 is inbound on the 71 route from Rubery and will turn to the left of the building between it and outward-bound car 560, on the 35 route short-working to Selly Oak.

In this bustling 1949 scene, the tramcar still appears to be the main mode of public transport, at least in this part of Birmingham. It seems as permanent as the sign for the products of the Rootes Group; the names Humber, Hillman, Sunbeam-Talbot, Commer and Karrier were to disappear in the 1960s and 1970s along with the building on which the hoarding stands. The rather down-at-heel Ford Ten Tudor on the left (meaning Two Door rather than of the period of Henry VIII!) looks as though it would not last much longer. It is passing Morrison Electricars VC40C two-ton dustcart 210, EVP 810, built in 1939, of the City of Birmingham Salvage Department. Perhaps surprisingly, it was the dustcart that would be the longest survivor in the photograph, as it would not be withdrawn until the mid-1960s. *F. N. Lloyd Jones*

Middle right In August 1951 car 802 has just turned from the Horse Fair into Bristol Street on its way to Rednal on the 70 route. In the far distance is a 1949 Daimler CVD6 with a Metro-Cammell body, working on a Special duty. These buses were some of the quietest and most refined of all Birmingham's post-war bus fleet and were popular with drivers and passengers alike.

All the buildings to the right of car 802 were demolished in the 1960s for the widening of Bristol Street and the Horse Fair to dual carriageways. This included the demolition of St Catherine of Sienna, a Victorian Gothic Roman Catholic church, built in the mid-19th century, but extended with an enlarged chancel in 1890. All the shops to the left of the tram still remain, although now they are mainly occupied by high-quality Indian restaurants. *R. T. Wilson*

Bottom right The Birmingham-registered 1936 Morris Twelve-Four is held up by trams 792 and 534, which are both leaving the city fully laden in Bristol Street, at its junction with Bromsgrove Street. In the distance an unidentified 762 Class car works inbound on the 70 route. With the exception of St Luke's church in the background, virtually all the buildings in this view remain today, including the splendid row of art nouveau shops just beyond car 534 in Bristol Street.

The selection of trams in this view represents the three main types of car used on the Bristol Road services during the last two years of operation. All have either 63 or 70 hp motors capable of maintaining well over 35 mph on the reserved track, while car 792 and the other eight-windowed tram are both equipped with EMB air brakes.

If there was a criticism of tramcar development by the Tramways Department it was that once the basic design of the Birmingham tram had been produced in 1913, with the 512 Class of bogie trams, the design development stagnated. Car 534 belongs to this earlier design, but in the course of rebuilding it became virtually indistinguishable from the later tramcars such as the eight-windowed car 792, which was built with only minor modifications some 15 years later. *R. T. Wilson*

Left After the takeover of the Bristol Road routes from the City of Birmingham Tramways Company on 1 July 1911, the Corporation's newest trams were used. As the former CBT depot at Bournbrook still contained the numerous sub-standard open-top cars and there was not enough room for any of the new stock, the routes along Bristol Road were at first operated partly from Moseley Road depot.

On a hot summer's day in 1911, not long after the BCT takeover, a lady with a parasol starts to cross Bristol Street near the junction with Belgrave Road. The distant tram is one of the newly introduced UEC-built 301 Class cars, still in original condition with the large offside vestibule window. The characteristic metal cowl, a well-known Birmingham feature necessary to give sufficient clearance over the brake handle, has not yet been fitted; for their first eight or so months in service the 301-360 batch of cars retained their original vertical handbrake handles, and it was only on being converted to horizontal handbrake wheels that the cars were altered.

It will be seen when comparing this view with that of 552 below, taken historically across the Great War divide, that the original CBT bracket arms were shorter, which necessitated the trams' trolleypole being extended over the kerb far more. *Commercial postcard*

Left Cloche-hatted women and straw-boatered and cloth-capped men go about their business in Bristol Street. It is the early 1920s, and this main road out of the city is a bustling commercial suburban shopping area. Although only about half a mile from the city centre it has the tree-lined prosperity generally lacking at that time on the other main roads into the city.

Brush-built tram 552, working the 36 route to Cotteridge and still in its original condition with open balconies, passes the junction with St Lukes Road beneath the delicate tracery of the overhead bracket supports. Although the Bristol Street route had the advantages of being double-track, the overhead was still suspended from the rather ornate side-bracket arms. By the middle of the 1920s this had generally been replaced by span wires. *Commercial postcard*

Right On page 68 of Volume 1 car 342 appeared towards the end of its career, working the 5 route in Victoria Road. Earlier in its working life it was allocated to Selly Oak depot, and is seen here on 26 November 1938 at the compulsory stop at Belgrave Road when working the 72 route, a short-working which went as far as Longbridge and the Austin Motor Works. 'The Armoured Car', as it was nicknamed, had been running since January 1921 with the prototype experimental design of covered vestibule. This had been fitted as a temporary measure, as totally enclosed, four-wheeled, double-deck tramcars were officially not allowed on narrow-gauge systems by the Board of Trade, because it increased their instability. Car 342 with its rather awkwardly styled balcony windows remained in service until 30 September 1950, but is seen here in the splendid post-1931 livery, fully lined out in blue and gold, although the earlier version also had the window pillars lined out. *L. W. Perkins*

BIRMINGHAM TRAMS 1933-53

Right Only one of the Washwood Heath bow-collector cars, 785, failed to live out a full working life. In April 1941 a bomb badly damaged cars 781, 785, 786 and 809 at the depot, having fallen between 785 and 786; the latter was kept throughout the remainder of the war before being repaired using parts from 785's good end. It re-entering service in February 1946 and, now fitted with a trolley pole after being transferred to Selly Oak depot in October 1950, crests the rise of Bristol Road at Wellington Road, just beyond the ABC Bristol Road Cinema which stood at the Spring Vale-Belgrave Road junction.

The tram is working the 71 route to Rubery, and this section went through land that was owned by the Calthorpe family; according to the novelist Francis Brett Young, the Calthorpe Estate was 'an area of tree-lined roads and exquisitely tasteful houses, tennis courts and croquet lawns, rose trees and rhododendron bushes. . .' The mid-19th-century houses to the right of the tram on the Balsall Heath side of the road were built to provide an area of good-quality housing along Bristol Road, but by the early 1950s they were falling into a fairly sorry state and would only survive until the end of the decade, being replaced by modern maisonettes and flats in the early 1960s. By way of contrast, on the extreme left is Wellington Road, one of the most prestigious addresses in Edgbaston where the Regency and early Victorian houses stood in their own grounds, reflecting an opulence that has been sustained only in this part of the Calthorpe Estate. *R. T. Wilson*

Middle right The original trams that opened the overhead electric tram service along Bristol Road were those owned by CBT. Car 152 was built in 1901 by the Electric Railway & Tramway Carriage Works and was an open-topped, reversed-staircase, double-decker, seating 48 and mounted on Packham 9A cantilever trucks. The class, numbered 151-165, had two BTH GE 58 6T motors, each of 28 hp.

Car 152 is seen in Bristol Road at Priory Road, Edgbaston, in about 1904, passing through the highly prosperous suburban arcadia of the Calthorpe Estate on its way to Bournbrook, where the original CBT accumulator trams terminated. CBT extended the route to the new electric tram terminus at Chapel Lane, Selly Oak, which was opened on 14 May 1901.

Car 152 was taken over by Birmingham Corporation Tramways in July 1911 and renumbered 502. It finally ran in service in December 1920, still in its open-top state; it was then converted to PW car 7 for use as a scrubber tram. It did not last long in this role, being broken up in June 1926. *Commercial postcard*

Bottom right Beyond Priory Road was the first section of reserved track in Bristol Road, and within 200 yards was the junction where the Cotteridge cars, working the 36 route, turned left into Pebble Mill Road. Car 742, one of the 1926 Brush-built EMB air-brake bogie cars, is on the inbound line just on the city side of this junction at the Bundy clocks that stood between the tram tracks in the middle of the central reservation. These were used by the platform staff to 'clock in'; they also recorded the time-keeping of the services, and were only phased out by West Midlands Passenger Transport in the 1980s.

The uniformed schoolchildren seem to be playing around. On today's A38 road such frolics would be virtually impossible, if not suicidal, as this is one of the busiest of Birmingham's main arterial roads. The Midland Red bus is a BMMO S8 with an MCCW body and is working the 145 route to Bromsgrove via West Heath and Barnt Green. *R. T. Wilson*

Left Car 630 speeds across the Pebble Mill Road junction on the 72 route on 25 June 1952. The conductor, with Bell Punch ticket machine and leather money bag strapped over his summer dust jacket, looks out of the entrance towards the approaching tram stop at the city end of the dual carriageway run from Selly Oak.

The tram is one of the 587-636 Class built by the Brush Electrical Engineering Company of Loughborough in 1920. It was built as a four-window, vestibuled-platform vehicle with open balconies and had Brush Burnley maximum traction bogies and GE 249A 37 hp motors. Birmingham's Tramway Department became interested in improving the braking performance of the tram fleet, and as a result car 630 was fitted with EMB Maley air brakes in June 1923, and later with the more powerful DK30/1L 63 hp motors. It was used as the prototype for the later air-brake bogie cars more usually associated with the Ladywood and Bristol Road routes; these were the 732-761 Class, built in 1926 and fitted from new with air brakes.

Latterly, 630 ran alongside the newer air-brake cars, being variously allocated to Rosebery Street, Washwood Heath and finally Selly Oak depots. It was always the odd one out amongst the air-brake bogie tram fleet, but unlike some 19 of the same 587 Class that survived until the final abandonment of the Birmingham system on 4 July 1953, car 630 was broken up with all the other surviving air-brake cars in July 1952 after the Bristol Road abandonment. *L. W. Perkins*

Left The pre-war livery, with its cream rocker panels and large shaded numerals, was replaced in 1946, and all the remaining enclosed bogie cars were repainted in the simplified post-war style. A fairly late survivor in the dignified earlier livery arrangement was car 744, photographed in August 1948 about to cross the gap in the central reservation where the Cotteridge-bound trams turned into Pebble Mill Road, which is off the photograph to the right.

This particular tram was one of the few of the 1926 Brush-bodied, EMB air-brake cars to be allocated to three depots. It was originally allocated to Rosebery Street depot for use on the Hagley Road and Ladywood services. In the 1930s it was also used at Selly Oak and Washwood Heath depots before finally settling at Selly Oak in January 1940. Unfortunately, 744 was involved in a severe accident in July 1942 and was stored in Sampson Road paint shop from November 1943 until June 1945. It had the distinction of being the only Birmingham tram stored there to escape the breakers' torch and be returned to service, still in the pre-war livery. *D. Griffiths*

Left The tree-lined central reservation track along sections of the Bristol Road enabled the bogie trams equipped with higher horsepower motors to achieve speeds of well over 40 mph. Car 587 was another of the 587-636 Class built by Brush in 1920 (see above left), and this photograph was taken about 30 years later, by which time the car's original motors had been replaced by Dick, Kerr DK 30/1 63 hp ones and its balconies had been enclosed. This car overturned in Suffolk Street in 1942 (see page 8), and no doubt as a result became one of nine of the class requiring to have its body strengthened. It was one of only 19 tramcars to be transferred in July 1952 for further service on the final Erdington group of routes, and was finally withdrawn on the last day of tramway operation in the city, 4 July 1953. *C. Carter*

Left Cars 781 and 737 stand forlornly on the Bristol Road reserved carriageway at Eastern Road on 8 July 1952, the Tuesday after the abandonment of the route. It had been decided to break up all the air-brake cars at Witton depot, but because it had a capacity of only about 40 trams, 54 cars, formerly allocated to Selly Oak and Cotteridge depots, were stored on this central reservation between Pebble Mill Road and Eastern Road, gradually being transferred to Witton depot as the breaking up got under way. The very last car to be removed, 513, was driven away for scrapping on 23 July 1952. There was a watchman on duty to guard the trams, but it is quite remarkable that virtually no vandalism took place throughout this period of storage down the middle of one of the main roads in Birmingham! However, the destination box and headlight of car 781 did disappear to a souvenir-hunter on the evening of the final closure. *T. J. Edgington*

Right The first electric tram route along Bristol Road was opened by the Birmingham Central Tramways Company on 24 July 1890, and was operated by the largest fleet of battery accumulator trams in the country, some 14 being used on the service between Suffolk Street and the Bournbrook terminus at Dawlish Road.

Cars 101-112 were eight-wheel bogie trams built by the Falcon Engine & Car Works of Loughborough and were very similar in design to the cable-cars that operated on the Snow Hill to Handsworth line. They seated 48 passengers and were operated from a depot in Dawlish Road, which was eventually taken over in 1911 by Birmingham Corporation.

Despite the problems of battery operation, which included sluggish performance and acid leaking from the batteries, the trams worked until replacement by conventional overhead electric cars on 14 May 1901. The pioneering nature of this experimental service, although not without its critics at the time, must have been reasonably successful, as it lasted for nearly 11 years!

Car 108 is seen in Bristol Road, Bournbrook, in CBT ownership in about 1897. The six hinged doors that contained the batteries form the rocker panel of the tram. *Dr H. W. Whitcombe collection, Science Museum, London*

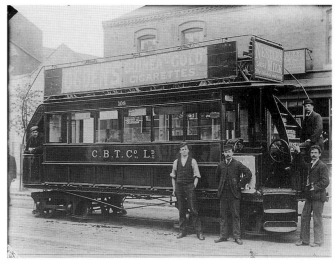

Right On a miserable Wednesday 12 April 1939, car 752 is about to leave the Dawlish Road compulsory stop in Bristol Road, on the climb up to Selly Oak, outside the Ten Acres & Stirchley Co-operative Society's (TASCO) grocery and provisions store. TASCO was a separate Co-operative Society in Birmingham and ran a chain of shops in the south-west of the city that remained independent of the nearby much larger Birmingham Co-operative Society until the early 1970s.

Car 752 belonged to the first class of 30 trams in Birmingham to be fitted with air brakes and was to serve the Bristol Road routes for about 19 years. It is in the standard, rather dignified pre-war lined-out livery and is working the 71 route to Rubery. *H. B. Priestley*

Selly Oak

Right On Thursday 5 May 1949 car 743 is passed by a Bedford van on the inside as it rushes towards Selly Oak. Bristol Road in Bournbrook was also known as High Street, and in the days of the City of Birmingham Tramways Co Ltd, which operated battery accumulator trams, the terminus was at the bottom of the hill at Dawlish Road. Car 743 has stopped on this hill between the original terminus and the Selly Oak terminus at Chapel Lane to which it was extended on 14 May 1901.

The tram is parked outside a teashop, which was the usual place for the crew to get their white enamel billy-can filled up with tea. The driver might drink a cupful whilst driving the tram; the rest would be consumed once the terminus was reached. Just behind the tram is the black and white gable-ended 'Friends' Institute', opened in 1894 at a cost of £5,500, which was donated by George Cadbury, the well-known chocolate manufacturer and philanthropist. *J. E. Cull*

Left A little beyond the 'Friends' Institute' was the railway bridge that took the Midland Railway's Birmingham and West Suburban railway line over the Bristol Road. It had a restricted height and the trams suitable for this route carried a cast metal plaque that read 'This car can run on Aston & Rednal routes' or 'Low Bridge Car. Selly Oak, Aston, Dudley Port' as appropriate.

Car 534, one of the GEC WT32R 70 hp re-motored trams, had been repainted in June 1949 and its well-varnished paintwork shines in the sunlight. In view of the fact that the tram had only two more years of service in front of it, it is surprising that it had its body strengthened after this, when overhauled on 23 June 1950. The tram is working the 71 route to Rubery and is about to go beneath the bridge on its way from the city, having just passed the stationary Morris-Commercial PV-type van. A Guy Vixen lorry is emerging from the shadows of the bridge. *Lens of Sutton*

Left Emerging from Selly Oak bridge, Brush-built EMB air-brake car 748 powers up the hill from Bournbrook while working the 71 route on 17 June 1952, towards the end of its 26-year service life. Note that its trolley-pole is extended to the kerb-side in order to become low enough to clear the bridge.

On the bridge is a large, scarcely missable advertisement for Dares Ales. Dares's South End brewery in Belgrave Road was taken over by the nearby Davenports in 1961; ironically its site, now in Belgrave Middleway, is today occupied by the Birmingham Central Mosque!

Beyond the bridge can be seen the imposing edifice of Birmingham University, opened on 7 July 1909 by King Edward VII and Queen Alexandra. Its almost Byzantine basilican-styled domed Great Hall, coupled with the just visible slender campanile which was modelled upon the 14th-century Torre del Mangia at Sienna, stand on a hill in Edgbaston. The distant academic heights are a world apart from the busy street scene with the advertisement for Joe Loss at the Birmingham Hippodrome offering a less cerebral type of entertainment. *R. Brook*

Right Cars 524 and 737, running into Selly Oak depot after the rush hour on an autumn day in 1951, have arrived from the outer terminus and reversed in order to turn into Chapel Lane.

This junction was dominated by three buildings, all of which offered in a variety of ways welcoming hospitality or entertainment. Opposite the road junction stood St John's Methodist Church, built in 1876 and closed for worship in about 1959. Next to the tram is the curved face of the Plough and Harrow public house, which had originally opened in 1900 as the New Inn. Behind the photographer was the 1,200-seat Oak Cinema, which opened in 1924 with a showing of *Chu Chin Chow*; only a few months before this photograph was taken it had been voted the second cleanest cinema in the country.

Alas, nearly all has gone today in a road-widening scheme that has largely removed the Selly Oak bottleneck on the Outer Ring Road and transferred it just down the hill towards the city in Bournbrook. The chapel was demolished in the late 1970s after being used for a number of non-secular functions; the Plough and Harrow went the same way in the early 1980s and the Oak was pulled down in December 1984. *R. T. Wilson*

Left A slightly unkempt car 784 turns into Bristol Road from Chapel Lane on the last morning of services to Rednal and Rubery. The few people walking about that day scarcely give the trams a second glance, but by the following morning their service would be operated by buses. It would not be quite the end for the former Washwood Heath bow-collector, Brush-built air-brake car of 1928, however; it would be stored on the Bristol Road central reservation from the cessation of the evening service until the final movements of trams along Bristol Road on Thursday 23 July, when along with 19 other trams it was driven to Kyotts Lake Road for scrapping (see also page 23). The only building to survive today is the Dog and Partridge public house, whose frontage, at least, looks early Victorian. *A. K. Terry*

Right A further view of the Plough and Harrow corner, with Harborne garage's AEC Matador 0853 No 14 involved in the recovery of the damaged vehicles when tramcar 595, a Brush-built car of 1920, was involved in an accident on 5 June 1950 with an ex-Army Austin K6 4x4. The accident blocked the Selly Oak junction for several hours. The ex-Royal Air Force Matador was acquired in January 1948, and although in this case it was carrying the trade plate 1620 O, it usually had the trade plate number 924 OP. After withdrawal it was acquired for preservation. *J. E. Cull*

Below Chapel Lane was only used for depot workings by the trams allocated to Selly Oak depot. On 7 June 1952 cars 767 and 518 have climbed the hill to join Bristol Road at the Selly Oak junction. To the left of the trams is the Oak Cinema, while behind tram 767, which is about to turn towards the city centre, is the Plough and Harrow.

Car 767 was one of the Brush-built, totally enclosed, EMB air-brake cars of 1928. It was mounted on EMB Burnley maximum traction bogies and was fitted with air-wheel, air-track and magnetic brake gear. Originally allocated to Washwood Heath depot, these trams' Dick, Kerr DK30/1L 63 hp motors and Fischer bow collectors allowed them to give some very spirited performances along Washwood Heath Road; yet when transferred to Selly Oak they were not as popular with the staff because of their complicated braking system.

Waiting at the bus stop in Chapel Lane while working on the 20 route to the City via the nearby Weoley Castle housing estate is 1545 (GOE 545), a Daimler CVA6 with an MCCW body, which entered service on 2 October 1947 and was to remain active until the last day of May 1962. *J. H. Meredith*

Middle left With its splendid Dutch-style gables and large entrance doors, Selly Oak depot had a capacity for about 80 trams on its ten roads. It was opened on 12 July 1927 and its capacity was a substantial improvement on the former CBT depot in Dawlish Road, Bournbrook, which had been opened in May 1901 and could only accommodate 46 trams. The extensions along Bristol Road from Selly Oak, to Northfield on 1 October 1923, to Longbridge on 17 December of the same year, to Rednal on 14 April 1924 and finally to Rubery on Monday 8 February 1926, meant that with a larger fleet of trams being required a bigger depot was needed. Selly Oak was built at the bottom of Chapel Lane in Harborne Lane and remained in operation as a tram depot until 5 July 1952, although it had been a bus garage as well since 2 January 1935.

On 24 February 1952 cars 519 and 743 stand on the forecourt of the depot in company with 1657 (HOV 657), the second of the 100 Leyland Titan PD2/1s of 1948-49, which like the two trams was bodied by the Brush company. The three single-deckers are Leyland Tiger PS2/1s with Weymann B34F bodies, which were delivered in 1950 to replace the pre-war fleet of Daimler COG5 single-deckers. The only one of the three that is identifiable, 2233 (JOJ 233), was to become the first member of the class to be withdrawn in 1962 after being hit by a fire engine in Northfield on 9 September 1961.

Just visible inside the depot is car 757. With its windows painted out, this tram was used as a cleaners' room until 14 May 1952 while the depot was being converted into a bus garage. *T. J. Edgington*

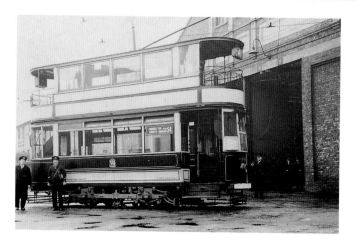

Left Former CBT car 240 was built at Kyotts Lake Road to a Brush design. New in 1904, it belonged to the class of trams known as the 'Aston' type; indeed, many of this type worked nearly all their Company careers on the Aston routes. Car 240, however, is known to have been at Bournbrook depot for a short time when nearly new, but by 1907 until the takeover of CBT by Birmingham Corporation on 1 January 1912, it was allocated, along with the other members of the class, to Witton. Some time after it had been taken into the BCT fleet it was renumbered 470. Originally it was an open-top car seating 26 on the outside and 22 in the lower saloon, and was fitted with Brush AA 6 ft 6 in wheelbase trucks and two 25 hp motors, but was totally rebuilt in 1925 to a vestibuled top-covered 35 hp tram. It stands at the entrance to road 7 at Selly Oak depot early in 1938, in its final form shortly before withdrawal from service. *W. A. Camwell*

Above The pollarded tree is not the Old Oak Tree from which Selly Oak got its name and which was felled in May 1909! It stands in front of a row of rather down-at-heel Victorian premises, a few of which were still being used as houses. The Stechford Fireplace & Plumbing shop displays one of its latest designs of stone fireplace, which were the height of suburban style until coal fires began to be phased out in the late 1950s, with the introduction of the Clean Air Act.

Short Brothers-bodied Cotteridge car 835 was used by Selly Oak depot on 16 May 1952 for about two weeks to cover for tram shortages on the Bristol Road routes. It is at the compulsory tram stop in Selly Oak, just past the junction with Chapel Lane, opposite which,in the background, stands St John's Methodist church, seen on page 25. *R. T. Wilson*

Below The village of Selly Oak was developed in the middle of the 19th century as a mixed industrial and residential area. The character of the suburb in the 1920s cannot have altered significantly since a large number of the Victorian buildings were still in residential use and not converted to retail outlets.

Car 375, working on the 35 route, stands at the Selly Oak tram terminus, which was to the south side of Chapel Lane and had replaced the original 1901 CBT terminus in 1923. In that year the route was extended along reserved track to the next important centre, the former village of Northfield. The tram has stopped opposite the Bundy clock and the driver, leaning against the tramcar, is waiting for the clock to come round to his departure time. In the foreground is the depot curve into Chapel Lane, which shows that the photograph was taken after July 1927 when Selly Oak depot was opened.

The tram was one of the United Electric Car Company's 40 hp four-wheelers of 1911. It was inherited by Selly Oak depot from Bournbrook in 1927, remaining there with only one small break until August 1938. After being allocated mainly to Coventry Road and Miller Street depots for the next 12 years, it was withdrawn in September 1950. It had the distinction of being the last standard four-wheel tram, other than the preserved car 395, to be moved across Birmingham when it was transferred from Kyotts Lake Road Works to Witton depot for scrapping in November 1950. *Commercial postcard*

Selly Oak to Northfield, Longbridge, Rednal and Rubery

Right An almost full car 798 coasts into the top southern end of Selly Oak at the Oak Tree Lane junction on its way into the city from Rednal. The car was one of the 762-811 Class built by Brush in 1928 and mounted on EMB Burnley maximum traction bogies. The arrangement of the wheels can be clearly seen in this view taken on 10 July 1951. The larger 31½-inch driving wheels were at the outer end of the bogie, and with the underframe of the tram resting over these driving wheels it meant that about 85 per cent of the car's weight of 16¾ tons was available for accelerating and braking. With a capacity of 60 passengers, the stability of these large, thin-looking trams was dependent upon the performance of the bogies when travelling at up to 40 mph on the narrow 3 ft 6 in gauge reserved track. *J. Cull*

Left The climb out of Selly Oak continued for a few hundred yards but soon reached the first stretch of reserved track that extended to the crest of Griffins Hill at Weoley Park Road. Car 775, another of the ex-Washwood Heath bow-collector cars transferred to Bristol Road workings in October 1950, leaves Selly Oak while working the 70 route from Rednal.

The nature of the surrounding area changed quite suddenly from the distant structural heights of the 19th century buildings to the mock-Elizabethan gabled semi-detached housing of the late 1920s. This was virtually the end of the housing development along Bristol Road until the edge of the suburb of Northfield was reached, just over two miles away. The intervening land was either owned by the Methodist Church's Selly Oak Colleges or by the Cadbury-owned Bournville Village Trust, and had generally been kept free of housing development. *R. F. Mack*

Left One of Cotteridge's Short Brothers-built trams, 833, was used by Selly Oak depot for its final six weeks of service, and is seen here having just left the tram stop on Bristol Road's reserved track at Witherford Way. It is working the 70 route on its way into the city and is just beginning the climb up Griffins Hill opposite Fircroft, a large Edwardian half-timber and brick house which was later converted to collegiate use in 1957 to become part of the Selly Oak teacher training colleges.

It is Saturday 5 July 1952 and the notices announcing the closure of the Bristol Road group of tram services are in the front balcony window. The somewhat reduced standards of track maintenance are visible as 833 kicks up dust as it accelerates towards the city. Beyond, at the top of the hill, the laying of pipes by the local civil engineering company of Whittakers has closed one of the carriageways leading to an early example of a 'contra-flow'. *R. T. Wilson*

BIRMINGHAM TRAMS 1933-53

Above With only six days to go before the Bristol Road route abandonment, car 620, built as an open-balconied tram by Brush in 1920, speeds along the central reservation. The tram is travelling towards the city from Rubery on the 71 route and has just left the Hole Lane stop. To the right, behind the trees, is the future site of Bournville Girls' Technical College, which was opened in October 1955. This tram was an all-electric car and was fitted with Dick, Kerr DK 301L 63 hp motors. It had been transferred from Miller Street on Thursday 19 June and would go back to the north side of the city on the day before the closure. *P. Jaques*

Right The rise out of the Griffins Brook valley between Selly Oak and Northfield was a steady, fairly slow climb for a fully laden 40 hp four-wheeler. The 301 Class, the backbone for many years of both Bournbrook and Selly Oak depots' tram fleets, was displaced by the more powerful re-motored 512 and 587 Classes of bogie cars in 1939.

Car 321, an open-balconied 1911 vintage tram, had been at Miller Street until March 1929 when it went to Selly Oak depot. It was transferred to Rosebery Street on 29 March 1939 and was later to become one of 50 of the class to be repainted during the Second World War in the drab grey livery. Here it is seen on the 72 route in the late 1930s at the Northfield end of the reserved track at Whitehill Lane. It is passing the then Royal Hospital for Crippled Children, which had formerly been a large private house known as the Woodlands; this in turn became The Royal Orthopaedic Hospital. *D. R. Harvey collection*

Right Car 734 enters the long section of reserved track at St Lawrence Road as it travels towards the city working the 70 route. This class of 30 EMB air-braked tramcars finished their 26 years in service working in the main from Selly Oak depot, although there was always the odd one or two allocated to Cotteridge. Car 734 looks as if the nearest platform has sagged a little under the strain of running at fairly high speed along Bristol Road's reserved track.

This splendid reserved track in Bristol Road South was a highlight of the Birmingham system and was comparable with any standard-gauge central reservation elsewhere in the country. *R. T. Wilson*

Left The transfer of the 587 Class of Brush-built all-electric bogie cars to Selly Oak depot, after the closure of the Hockley and West Bromwich routes in April 1939, helped to maintain the service frequency on the busy south-western route along Bristol Road. All of the class were re-motored with Dick, Kerr DK 30/1L 63 hp motors in the late 1920s, which made them compatible with the 732 Class that was fitted with EMB air-track brakes.

Car 623 had been a Selly Oak car almost continuously since Hockley depot had closed. It is standing at the Bundy clock in Northfield on the section of street track on the city side of the shopping centre outside the early-20th-century premises of Daniel & Son when working the 71 route in early 1952. The last building in the distance with the tall chimneys is the Travellers Rest public house which, rather incongruously, was built in the 1920s in a mock-Cotswold style surmounted with a thatched roof! *R. T. Wilson*

Left The Bristol Road routes, beyond the Inner Circle bus route at Belgrave Road, have retained their character since the abandonment of this part of the Birmingham tram system on 5 July 1952. In August 1993 preserved ex-Birmingham City Transport Crossley DD42/7 2489 (JOJ 489) was driven through Northfield and photographed in the same position as tram 623. In the intervening 41 years the buildings have remained remarkably untouched by redevelopment. The grocers with the sunblind extended in the earlier picture has become the Omar Khayam restaurant, while Daniel & Son is now a bookmakers. Unfortunately, in the rush to get a photograph of the Crossley in roughly the same position as tram 623, the destination blind on the bus was incorrectly matched to the route number, displaying 71 REDNAL instead of 71 RUBERY. So much for authenticity! *D. R. Harvey*

Right Strengthened 1913 Brush-built tram 517 leads the 15-years-newer 792 across the traffic lights at the Bell Hotel junction, both working on the 70 route from the city. The extent of the body rebuilding can be seen on the older tram as the bulkhead window and the adjacent lower saloon ventilator were plated over with quarter-inch-thick steel plates. Also waiting at the traffic lights is an almost new Austin Devon A40 four-door saloon with a nearly new motorist, judging by the 'L' plates.

The buildings behind the vehicles on the Church Road side of Bristol Road South were demolished in the early 1960s, but the replacement shops lay unfinished for many years. Eventually the Grosvenor shopping centre was completed which today dominates this junction. *D. R. Harvey collection*

Right In Birmingham, as in most large cities, directions are given by the location of notable landmarks such as crossroads, churches, important shops, but most commonly by the names of local public houses. Northfield had three of note on the main Bristol Road. Before the shopping centre on the city side was the aforementioned Travellers Rest. On the Longbridge side was the Black Horse, which was an excellent copy of a Tudor half-timbered manor house. In the background here, in the midst of the shopping centre, was the Bell Hotel, a rather ornately gabled and towered Edwardian hostelry, standing on the corner of Bell Lane.

At the time of the pub's construction, the old village of Northfield lay relatively undisturbed away from the main road route which went to Bromsgrove, just over one mile away to the south-east; as a result the whole of the area retained its agricultural nature. In fact, for many years after its construction the land next door to the Bell was occupied by the barns and out-houses of a farm. Today the site is occupied by a much smaller, 1980s-built Bell public house and a McDonald's restaurant. On Saturday 7 June 1952 car 798 waits to leave the Northfield clocking-in point on its way to Navigation Street while working the 70 route. *R. B. Parr*

Right The problems caused by picking up and setting down passengers without the benefit of kerb-side loading are very well demonstrated in this scene on the final Saturday morning in the centre of Northfield. Brush air-brake car 775 stands opposite the Bell Hotel, marooned by its own inflexibility in the middle of the road, while an Ansells brewery Leyland Comet is held up by the milling passengers. It is fortunate for the tram users that the amount of private car traffic, in the early postwar years, was so light. There had been considerable criticism of the traffic bottlenecks at Selly Oak and Northfield from the 1920s, and the role played by the trams in the potential congestion was criticised even then.

Car 775 would not be used after the end of this day, but was stored on the central reservation of the Bristol Road for some 13 days before being driven away for scrapping at Witton. *R. Knibbs*

Right The busy suburb of Northfield was surprisingly poorly covered by photographers, who seemed to prefer the outer termini of Bristol Road. However, here car 627 is caught crossing the turnback points used by the 69 route trams when they reached the splendidly turreted Bell Hotel. The tram is working on the 70 route and is travelling northwards towards the city in the summer of 1952. Just 18 months before this photograph was taken, Selly Oak depot had seven 587 Class trams numbered in the 620 sequence; of these, only car 627 survived the mass withdrawals of September 1950 and remained in regular service at Selly Oak depot for the Bristol Road services.

Picking up passengers on the 71 route to Rubery is air-brake bogie car 743, carrying the popular '3-in-One Oil' advertisement. Yet again the stream of passengers in the roadway shows the disadvantages of the absence of kerb-side loading. *Lens of Sutton*

BIRMINGHAM TRAMS 1933-53   31

Left Another of Northfield's distinctive public houses was the Black Horse at the corner of Bristol Road South and Frankley Beeches Road, built to the design of C. E. Bateman in 1929 for Davenports brewery. It was constructed in the form of a mock-Tudor manor house and hardly missed a trick in persuading the passer-by that it was not genuine; despite its youth, it is now a Grade II listed building.

Car 764 passes the pub on its way towards the city when working the 70 route in April 1952. Parked next to the Black Horse is the Morris Series Y-type 10 cwt van belonging to Bradfords, the large local bakers based opposite West Bromwich Albion's Hawthorns football ground. Beyond the tram in the distance are two early examples of articulated lorries, the nearer one being a wartime Bedford OW type. The distant Frankley Beeches Road was used by the 18 and 23 bus routes at this time to serve the Allens Cross municipal housing estate. *F. N. Lloyd Jones*

Right Strengthened Brush-built car 549 climbs Pigeon House Hill, Bristol Road South, on 5 July 1952 when running from the Longbridge direction on the 69 route short-working to Northfield. Until the mid-1930s this section of Bristol Road South was still farmland, and the only settlements beyond Northfield were at Tessall, at the bottom of the hill, which consisted of a few houses around a crossroads, and Longbridge.

Behind the tram, turning into South Road across the tram tracks and the central reservation, is an early post-war Morris Series Y 10 cwt van belonging to Royal Mail. Car 549 was one of only two trams in the fleet, the other being MRCW car 645, to display the balcony-dash advertisement 'Pond for Tools', which it carried for over 16 years. This tram would not be broken up after the closure of the Bristol Road group of routes but would see out another year's service at Miller Street. It was one of the last 23 to be scrapped during August 1953. *A. Yates*

Left In the summer of 1952 car 795, one of the 1928 totally enclosed 63 hp trams that were built by Brush, approaches the Austin factory, just visible behind the large trees on the left of the central reservation. To the right can be seen the extension to the Austin West Works, which was being constructed by the newly formed British Motor Corporation.

This particular tram was used in experiments by the EMB company to solve the problem of the slow wheel-brake auto-valve release mechanism. With Metropolitan Electric car 350, nicknamed 'Poppy', it was fitted with a simple and cheap cam-operated arrangement that allowed the air-wheel brake to be exhausted mechanically when the air-track brake was applied, which improved the driver's control over the braking as compared to the rest of the 762 Class. Car 795 was made standard with the rest of the class in 1941. *R. F. Mack*

Right Car 750 crests the railway bridge over the Halesowen branch line on 7 June 1952. The Halesowen Railway, opened on 10 September 1883 as a joint venture between the Great Western and Midland companies, left the latter's main line at Longbridge and had intermediate stations at Rubery and Hunnington before connecting with the GWR's branch line at Halesowen. The line should have become an important southern access route around the growing industrial West Midlands area, but unfortunately the line, for all its potential usefulness, had its Achilles' heel at Dowery Dell. Here a 660-foot-long cast iron trestle viaduct took the line over a 100-foot-deep valley. There was a 10 mph speed limit and a weight restriction in force that severely limited the types of locomotives that could be used over the fragile viaduct.

Although it later was used to bring Austin car workers in to the Longbridge factory from the Black Country, the Halesowen line was never a success and was eventually shut, with the formal closure taking place on 6 January 1964. The station used by the Austin car workers was to the west of the bridge over which tram 750 is passing. The workman's services that terminated at Longbridge were introduced as part of the First World War armaments drive and continued for another 40 years. Interestingly, this Longbridge station was never mentioned in any public timetable, despite having its booking and enquiry office staffed by British Railways officials. *H. B. Priestley*

Right The imposing iron shelters on the central reservation outside Austin's Longbridge factory in Lickey Road were designed to accommodate the thousands of car workers who swarmed on to the awaiting trams at the end of each shift. Car 534 stands on the reserved track outside the factory on 3 June 1952 before leaving for the 70 terminus at Rednal.

In 1905 Herbert Austin left the Wolseley Sheep Shearing Machine Company to set up his own car manufactory in some derelict premises that had made and colour-printed tin containers. This had been opened in 1894 by the Birmingham printers White & Pike, but the company hit financial difficulties in 1902 and vacated the site. Austin and his partners, Frank Keyser and Harvey Du Cros, purchased the premises at Longbridge on 10 November 1905. The factory was on the south side of the Halesowen Railway branch line, and to the east side of Bristol Road South under which the railway passed.

As early as July 1913 Birmingham Corporation had bought ten Daimler 40 hp motor-buses to act as feeders to the Selly Oak tram route to take the Austin car workers to the factory. Gradually the pull of this labour to Longbridge encouraged housing developments beyond Northfield towards the south-west. By the early 1920s the buses of the day were not able to cope with the increasing demands of the Austin works, so on 17 December 1923 the 72 service finally replaced the buses to Longbridge. *A. N. H. Glover*

Right The climb from Longbridge up Lickey Road to the Rednal terminus was just over a mile long, and progressed from the industrial landscape at the bottom of the hill through a long horse-chestnut-lined central reservation, before reaching Cofton Park. The park was open farmland until it was made public in 1936; it was originally known as High Park. The parked Austin Seven Ruby car is the only identifiable car in sight; it was made in the factory about half a mile away.

Car 796 is working on the 70 route on 3 June 1952; it is passing Edgewood Road, having travelled one stop from the tram terminus at Rednal. This former village had become part of

the city in 1911 and in contrast to the newly grown suburbia had a distinctly 'touristy' feel about it as it catered for all the summer tram-borne day-trippers.

This member of the 762 Class had been modified so that its EMB air-

wheel and air-track brakes could be applied at the same time. This proved popular with the motormen, producing a jerk-free and more positive braking action, but was removed in August 1941 after nearly 11 years of service because it was non-standard. *A. N. H. Glover*

Above On arrival at Rednal, the track crossed the carriageway at the top of the hill at Lickey Road opposite The Hare and Hounds public house and entered the 200-yard loop at the terminus. Car 528 is leaving the central reservation in Lickey Road on a sunny day in the summer of 1951. The driver can be seen looking into his mirror for any vehicles that might be approaching. It appears that the only car near to him, a 1937 Austin Ten, is stationary.

Car 528 was one of the 67 of the 512 Class of 1913 to survive the Second World War. Of these, 25 had been re-motored in 1927 with GEC WT32R 70 hp motors. All of the surviving 70 hp cars were rewired and had their bodies strengthened in about 1948 and evidence for this can be seen on car 528 as the bulkhead window on the platform has been plated over. *S. J. Eades*

Below Numerically the last of Moseley Road's allocation of half a dozen 301 Class trams, car 389 has just arrived at Rednal on the 709 route in the summer of 1949. In the background car 548 heads a line of trams waiting to leave the terminus. The short-trousered boys glance at the elderly, open-balconied tram, while the Inspector, holding a point bar in his right hand, looks at the track just in front of the tram. He was also employed to direct cars into the loop or the stub terminus as he deemed appropriate.

In the summer months Moseley Road depot supplied extra trams to augment the normal service cars operated by Selly Oak depot. They would start at the Queen's Hotel end of Navigation Street and use the cross-over into John Bright Street which was only otherwise used for journeys to Kyotts Lake Road Works. At the end of the Lickey Hills summer season in 1949, this manoeuvre by Moseley Road cars over the cross-over stopped and was not reintroduced as the Moseley Road group of tram routes closed at the beginning of October. *P. Jaques*

Right In December 1944 grey-painted car 525 caught fire at the Rednal terminus, allegedly because of an electrical cable fault; although the body was gutted by the fire, the trucks and controllers were later salvaged for further use. Here the forlorn remains of the car stand where the fire took place on the loop. The grey livery, the headlight masks and the wartime white edgings to the fenders and the body have largely survived the conflagration, but the interior fittings and apparently every pane of glass have been totally destroyed. After the fire the remains went back to the car's home depot at Selly Oak, where they were stored for several months. The tram was finally broken up in Sampson Road Paint Shop, the depository of a number of the wartime tramcar casualties and also the 16 Nechells trolleybuses that had been withdrawn on 1 October 1940. *BCT*

Above In addition to its well-known use, the terminal loop was used for stabling 18 trams as Selly Oak depot's allocation was more than its capacity. Car 788 is the last of the ten parked trams visible at the terminus, all with their trolleypoles tied down. The terminal loop was laid out on a grandiose scale to cater for the hundreds of passengers who would only have to spend up to fivepence for the ride out to the 950-foot-high Lickey Hills. There they could enjoy the 'Brummies' playground, which had been donated initially by the generosity of the Cadbury family in 1906, with country walks through a mixture of open parkland and picturesque arboreal glades, as the hills provided a cheap escape into the countryside. The decline of the tourist trade at the Lickeys began with the increase in post-war car ownership - the pleasant walks in the countryside became less attractive when a coach trip to Weston-super-Mare or Rhyl came within the financial grasp of the pre-war visitors. The abandonment of the trams, and this post-war increase in car ownership, sounded the end for the Lickey Hills as a major day-trip attraction. *W. J. Wyse*

Above With the trees starkly standing against the sky, devoid of their foliage above the impressive tram shelters at Rednal, car 344 stands empty on 6 January 1938 at the 70 route terminus. The shelters were constructed in 1925 at the same time as the loop line in order to cater for the large numbers of day-trippers who would board their tram back home after a day walking across the Lickeys. For a short time before this, the terminus had been temporarily located near Leach Green Lane.

The tram is one of the 301 Class that was constructed by UEC in 1911, and except for the later enclosed balconies on all the bogie cars built from car 637 onwards, this class set the design for all subsequent Birmingham tramcars. They were the first to have enclosed vestibules from new as well as having three-sided dash panels. This open-balcony, low-height, 52-seater tram was one of about 60 of the basically similar 301 and 361 Classes that were allocated to Selly Oak depot throughout the 1930s. When the Dudley and West Bromwich routes closed at the beginning of April 1939 it had enormous knock-on effects regarding tram allocation; a mass exodus of the four-wheelers occurred from Selly Oak, with car 344 leaving in May 1939. It was finally withdrawn in September 1950, being one of the last five four-wheelers to operate from Washwood Heath depot. *H. B. Priestley*

Left On its way back to the city from Rubery, car 781 negotiates the traffic island at Longbridge junction outside the Austin factory. The two main routes diverged at this point; the 70 route to Rednal continued off the right-hand side of the photograph, while the 71 route followed the Rubery branch, which 781 is leaving. This tram, with just a hint of a sagging platform, is a 1928 EMB air-brake car built by Brush and is carrying the '3-In-One Oil' advertisement. This was on the balcony panels of well over 100 trams in the last few years of operation, having been introduced in July 1951. *W. J. Wyse*

Right On a hot summer's day in July 1952 60-seater, Brush-built car 735 leaves the Rubery branch along Bristol Road South, beginning to emerge from the reserved island track before starting the climb over the railway bridge towards Northfield and the city. The row of utility-style Midland Red bus shelters just beyond the island to the left of the tram show that it was not just the Birmingham tram fleet that was required to move the Austin workers every day; Midland Red's service to Bromsgrove via Rubery village had a large part to play in the works services.

The carriageway and central reservation on Bristol Road South look much the same today as they did in 1952; it is the adjacent land use on either side of the road that has altered. Maisonettes were built in the late 1950s near the bus shelters and the wooden-hut-style Longbridge Assembly Rooms opposite, on the extreme right and in the picture below, have been replaced by what is today a Rover Cars training school. The one major change from the 1950s is that the wide and spacious dual carriageway road that was empty then is still able to cope with the demands of the traffic of the 1990s, a testimony perhaps to the foresight of the town planners of the post-Great War period. *A. Yates*

Right Another view of the junction as car 559 leaves Bristol Road South, passing the pumping station in the background. It is 3 June 1952 and this strengthened Brush-built car of 1913 would be one of the trams to survive the Bristol Road abandonment and be transferred to Miller Street depot for a further year's use on the remaining Aston Road group of routes. It is carrying the full post-war simplified livery, which although not as ornate as the lined-out pre-1946 style, did have a certain dignified charm, especially when the tram was in newly painted condition. Birmingham's trams always carried advertisements, although not every tram was so adorned. Car 559 carries advertisements that would please the 1950s housewife - on the front balcony panels it carries the slogan that 'Bovril puts beef into you', while the 'New Weekly Wash Sensation' of Tide, a product introduced in October 1951, mops up the Bovril stains afterwards! *A. N. H. Glover*

BIRMINGHAM TRAMS 1933-53

Right The rain glistens on the roofs of the interwar shops on the corner of Bristol Road South and Cliff Rock Road as totally enclosed EMB air-brake car 746 climbs up the gentle ascent from Longbridge towards the terminus of the 71 route at Rubery. The Rubery extension was the last to be completed as part of the Bristol Road extension and improvement schemes of the 1920s, being opened on 8 February 1926. Only the route extensions to Short Heath, Pype Hayes, Hall Green, Stechford and Fort Dunlop would be built after this date, and all but the last used reserved track along arterial routeways. This early 1951 view shows that the tramway reservation was an integral part of the interwar thinking about town planning in Birmingham, being at the centre of a tree-lined 120-foot dual carriageway. Today, as the cars and buses queue in Bristol Road South as they come from the nearby M5 motorway and struggle in ever increasing congestion towards Longbridge and Northfield, the wide grassed central strip stands in mute testimony to the concept of fast and economical high-speed trams on sleeper-laid, ballasted track. *W. J. Wyse*

Right The last of the 732 Class cars, tram 761 approaches the last quarter of a mile of the 71 route on the same miserable day as the previous photograph. This tram operated some 850,000 miles in its 26-year operating life. By way of comparison, albeit not quite fair as passenger loadings were much higher, in 1970 West Midland PTE used over 50 of the 3881-3980 Class of 33-foot-long Daimler Fleetline CRG6LXs on virtually the same routes. By 1981 all these buses had been withdrawn, mainly because their bodies were deteriorating so badly! *W. J. Wyse*

Below Standing at the Rubery terminus of the 71 route in the later days of the Second World War is car 551. It is fitted with masks on the headlights, and also visible is the small wartime rear light assembly mounted in a small box structure with the exposed wiring passing down behind the fender. This arrangement was altered to the more permanent Sanders lights

fitted after the war. The tram also has the fenders painted white; this was to make its edges more visible during the blackout, although realistically, with so little street and vehicle lighting available, the trams' near invisibility made little difference to other road users; they were also groping around in the darkness looking for other vehicles to avoid in the blackness. Vehicle lighting restrictions were lifted in Birmingham on 6 January 1945. The tram also carries the uncommon, late-wartime advertisement 'Victory Will Be Sweeter With Mars'.

Car 551 was experimentally fitted in July 1928 with a bow collector prior to their introduction on the Washwood Heath air-brake bogie cars. After the successful introduction of the 762 Class with their bow collectors, car 551 reverted to being fitted with the normal trolleypole and Boot design of trolley wheel. In January 1928 this was one of ten of the 512 Class to be fitted with the new design of top cover, which had an eight-window upper saloon to the same design as the contemporary 762 Class. *R. Elliott*

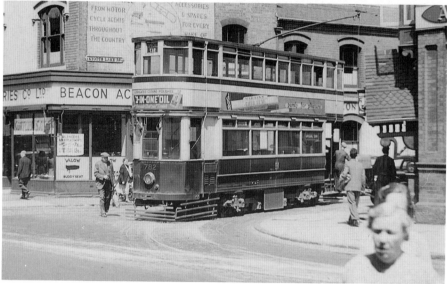

Left The sight of lightweight car 842 working away from its normal Cotteridge haunts was unusual, but in this case it was being used on a Light Railway Transport League (LRTL) tour on Saturday 7 June 1952. It stands waiting behind Brush air-brake car 752, which in turn waits for similar tram 744 to leave the single section of track adjacent to the Bundy clock. The comparison between the modern-looking 842 and the other two trams gives the impression that the nearer, traditional-looking trams belong to another generation of tramcar construction - in fact, cars 744 and 752 are only three years older! Although not as impressive as the Rednal terminus, the open spaces outside Rubery Hill Hospital might have supported a similar turning loop, but the terminal stub arrangement as the end of the reserved track seemed adequate enough to cope with the tram traffic. J. H. Meredith

Above From the early afternoon of 5 July 1952 during the final day of operation of the Bristol Road and Cotteridge routes, tramcars were selected for duties that terminated at the city centre terminus at Navigation Street. Once they had completed their last city-bound duty, their destination blinds were wound round to 'Special Car' for the last time and they made their journey to Kyotts Lake Road for storing. This process was applied to five of Cotteridge's trams and to ten of those allocated to Selly Oak depot, including car 782. They were all transferred to Witton depot for breaking up.

This tram, once one of Washwood Heath depot's proud bow-collector fleet, is seen reversing, under the watchful eye of one of the works staff who is riding on the platform, into Kyotts Lake Road on this final Saturday.

The Transport Committee had seen Birmingham trams as increasingly outmoded and anachronistic for over 20 years. Although the Second World War delayed the inevitable, events like this were seen as progress, with Birmingham's reputation for its 20th-century industry based on car manufacturing seemingly at odds with apparently archaic-looking trams rumbling through its streets. The abandonment plans, much delayed and altered as a consequence of the war, meant that the later air-brake-tram-operated routes became the penultimate group to be scrapped, in preference to the Aston Road services which were operated by the easier to maintain, slower, all-electric tramcars whose bodies were in better condition.

Thus it was that car 782, along with 107 other high-horsepower or air-brake trams went for scrap. The following month it would be driven across the city to Witton depot where it would finally be broken up. L. W. Perkins

Above On the evening of that Saturday, 5 July 1952, tram 777 closed the Bristol Road route. It finally reached Selly Oak depot in the early hours of Sunday morning at about the same time as car 800 was becoming the last tram into Cotteridge depot. The closure of the Bristol Road service was marked by the Transport Department using a tram with a fairly memorable fleet number. Car 777, one of the former bow-collector trams allocated for so many years to Washwood Heath depot, ran a complete round trip from Navigation Street to Rednal before returning to Selly Oak depot. By the next day, it and 53 other trams from Selly Oak and Cotteridge depots were parked on the central reservation near Eastern Road awaiting their next and final move to Witton for breaking up by W. T. Bird of Stratford-upon-Avon. D. R. Harvey collection

PERSHORE ROAD AND COTTERIDGE

THE Kings Norton and Northfield Urban District Council obtained the necessary powers to build an electric overhead tramway along Pershore Road to Cotteridge in 1901. The route of the new line was linked to the City of Birmingham Tramways Bristol Road route via Pebble Mill Road. As a result of this inevitable integration with the existing CBT system, the Urban District Council approached the tramway company to work the line on their behalf to Cotteridge.

The Birmingham boundary at that time was marked by Bournbrook, so that the quarter-mile section from Bristol Road along Pebble Mill Road to the bridge on Pershore Road opposite Cannon Hill Park was laid by Birmingham Corporation, as it was within its boundary, but at the expense of Kings Norton and Northfield UDC. The Corporation then let the line to the UDC for a nominal rent.

The Pershore Road service was opened between the stub terminus in Suffolk Street via Bristol Road and Pebble Mill Road as far as the temporary terminus near Mayfield Road, Stirchley, on 20 May 1904, although the CBT trams displayed the destination of Breedon Cross. The line was extended to Cotteridge on 23 June 1904.

The CBT open-top cars used on the route were from the 189-192, 193-208, 209-216 and 239-242 Classes, although other cars, including the converted bogie cars, 181-188, were undoubtedly used at Cotteridge depot. After it was opened in late June 1904 with an allocation of just eight trams, Cotteridge was regarded by the CBT Company as just an outstation for Bournbrook depot. There was a considerable amount of interchange of rolling-stock between the two depots as there was no separate allocation of tramcars. Rather surprisingly this situation continued throughout the years of Corporation operation, which accounts for the regular appearance of odd Selly Oak cars at Cotteridge depot and vice versa.

CBT had obtained a 21-year lease on the operation of the Bristol Road route which was due to expire in 1911, and the Pershore Road was to expire on the same date. The electrification agreement of 21 July 1900 allowed for Birmingham Corporation to purchase all the tram rolling-stock, electrical feeders and overhead within the city boundary on 1 July 1911; it duly took over on that date, at first on behalf of Kings Norton, until on 9 November

1911 Kings Norton Urban District, along with Aston Manor, Erdington, Handsworth, Northfield and Yardley, became part of Greater Birmingham.

The Pershore Road route and Cotteridge depot thereupon became solely owned by BCT. Thus it was that some 20 trams were transferred to BCT in July 1911, and a further 41 were similarly taken over with the purchase of the remainder of the CBT system at the end of the year.

The Pershore Road route as operated by both CBT and later the Corporation trams left Bristol Road via Pebble Mill Road. This was originally a narrow road through

Pershore Road and Cotteridge routes

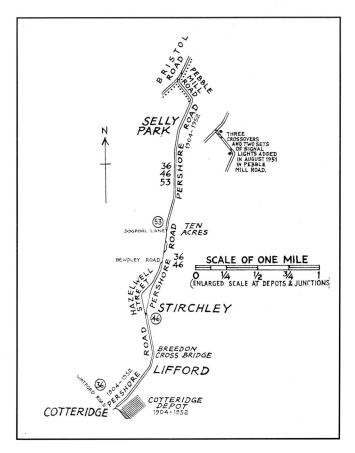

open land, but in 1919 it was to become something of a trail blazer as it was selected to be rebuilt as the prototype of the new arterial road system in the city with a central reservation capable of carrying tramcars.

At the junction with Pershore Road opposite Cannon Hill Park, the trams turned right and crossed the old city boundary at the Bournbrook bridge and into Selly Park. From here the tram route followed Pershore Road to the terminus at Cotteridge.

The gentle climb through Selly Park passed initially through a residential area of late-19th-century housing, although opposite Kensington Road there were a few attractive terraced houses from the early 1840s.

On reaching Kitchener Road the route turned slightly south-westwards and continued past a long row of large, distinctive early-20th-century terraced housing.

The former hamlet of Ten Acres was reached about one and quarter miles from Pebble Mill road. After the track was doubled in 1914, Ten Acres became the first main turnback point along the route; in later years, this became the short-working from the city, numbered 53. Ten Acres was at the junction with Dogpool Lane, and beyond this was a section of single-line track that was about a quarter of a mile in length with a passing loop. This narrow piece of roadway had houses and industry on either side; historically this had its origins in the industrial mills associated with the nearby Griffins Brook and the River Rea.

Once Griffins Brook had been crossed, the route arrived at Stirchley. Here the route split, only the outward line continuing along Pershore Road. The inward route followed Hazelwell Street from the bifurcation opposite the British Oak at the rather solid-looking, turn-of-the-century Church of the Ascension northwards past the bottom on Bournville Lane, on whose corner was the swimming baths and the library. On the east side, opposite Bournville Lane, was the original site of George Cadbury's first Day Release College, which was opened in the 1890s. After curving to the right Pershore Right was regained at Umberslade Road just short of the Three Horseshoes public house and outside the departmental store and headquarters of the Ten Acres and Stirchley Co-operative Society.

Immediately after the two sections rejoined at the British Oak public house, the busy Victorian suburban shopping centre of Stirchley Street was reached. At the far end of these shops, for the first six weeks of the line's operation, was the temporary Breedon Cross terminus, actually some distance away, north of Fordhouse Lane.

Beyond the end of this straight quarter-mile-long section of street track, the route climbed and twisted sharply over Breedon Cross bridge. This took the tram tracks over the Worcester & Birmingham Canal and a little-used railway line, to reach the Breedon Cross public house, which dominated the southbound exit from the bridge, and past the Savoy cinema.

The line resumed its steady climb towards Cotteridge. It went up a short hill to Frances Road, passing Cotteridge School on the right and rows of better quality Victorian terraces on the left.

The final quarter of a mile took the route past more late-19th-century houses and shops as well as crossing two railway bridges before curving away through the Edwardian shopping centre of Cotteridge, dominated by St Agnes's Church. At the far end of the shops, at Watford Road, the terminus was finally reached opposite Cotteridge depot, access to which was from the single terminal stub line.

The 36 route to Cotteridge allowed for a certain amount of high-speed running, and after the First World War bogie cars were the normal type on the route. In later years the newest of the traditional-looking Birmingham trams, the 812 Class of M&T bogie cars, were always associated with the service along Pershore Road. Added to the Pershore Road route's regular trams were the two lightweight cars, 842 and 843, which were the last trams purchased by the Corporation. After 1930 the depot allocation at Cotteridge remained remarkably stable.

Navigation Street to Pebble Mill Road

Top right The Pershore Road tram route, in common with those along Bristol Road, began at Navigation Street, and used the loop around Navigation Street and John Bright Street that had been introduced on 4 February 1902 for the CBT's electric trams working on Bristol Road to Bournbrook. This was some nine months after this route had been converted from the unreliable battery-accumulator tramcars on 14 May 1901, and the loop replaced the terminal stub in Suffolk Street and enabled the electric cars to get a little nearer to the centre of Birmingham without the awkward manoeuvres involved in reversing.

The Pershore Road route opened on 20 May 1904, thus post-dating the original CBT terminus. At first the service only went as far as Stirchley and the route had to be operated by Bournbrook depot, but after the route was extended to Cotteridge on 23 June 1904 and a small depot opened at the Cotteridge terminus, the workings were shared between the two depots until 1920. The route remained unaltered until its final closure.

Cars 826, 623, 605 and 812 stand in Navigation Street just above the loading shelters on 3 June 1950. Cars 826 and 812 were built by Short Brothers Ltd, of Rochester, Kent, mounted on standard Brush underframes. These trams were associated almost exclusively with the Pershore Road route, and these two worked right up until the last day of Cotteridge operation. Brush-built car 623 was destined to be one of the two cars that finally closed the Birmingham system. Identical tram 605 was not so fortunate, being one of 26 of the 587 Class to be withdrawn, when the EMB air-brake members of the 762 Class were transferred to Selly Oak depot upon the closure of the Washwood Heath routes on 30 September 1950. Car 605 was broken up at Witton by December of the same year. *J. H. Meredith*

Middle right The experimental Short Brothers-bodied lightweight tram 842 stands at the Navigation Street loading shelters working on the 36 route in June 1949. It was constructed using parts provided by Aluminium (TI) Ltd, Shorts and the Transport Department, who shared the development and construction costs of the vehicle over and above the normal price for a compositely constructed Birmingham Corporation tramcar.

Car 842 entered service on 28 November 1929. With its domed roof, flush sides and four-bay construction, it was the most radically different-looking tramcar to enter service in the city. It was also fitted with English Electric lightweight steel bogies, which had 26-inch diameter driving wheels and 20-inch diameter pony wheels. This was one of the main reasons why this tramcar was the lowest top-covered tram in the BCT fleet at 15 ft 6 in. This photograph was taken when this unique tram was still fitted with its original bogies, which were later replaced by the Maley & Taunton ones from the withdrawn car 821 in November 1950. One of the hoardings in the tram shelter was advertising that the West End cinema was showing *The History of Mr Polly*, starring John Mills in a 1949 adaptation of H. G. Wells's novel. *R. Marshall*

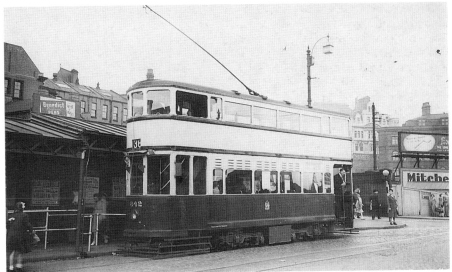

Bottom right The little girl looks on with interest from the window beneath the side destination box as three women alight at the Horsefair unloading island from car 820, working the 36 route on 21 June 1952. This unloading island was removed just one week before the abandonment of the tram services so that the replacement buses would not be obstructed.

Before the start of the construction of Smallbrook Queensway on 8 March 1957, the Horse Fair and the nearby small-scale shopping area of Smallbrook Street were far more accessible for pedestrians. Smallbrook Street also allowed access to the markets area and to New Street Station. However, this was all before the boom in car ownership and the consequent decline of public transport as a prime mover of people. The Singer Bantam car in the distance is the only other vehicle on an otherwise deserted city centre street. Within a few years it was deemed necessary to rebuild the street system as the exiting road pattern could be seen as becoming too congested and unable to cope with the increase in car ownership. What was thereby lost was the urban landscape and road systems that had been inherited from the late Victorian growth of the city.

Car 820 was the only one of the Short Brothers-bodied Maley & Taunton air-brake cars to be strengthened; it re-entered service in November 1950 having had its bulkhead windows plated over in the same way that some 56 older trams had been. This modification can clearly be seen above the head of the first woman leaving the tramcar. *J. Cull*

BIRMINGHAM TRAMS 1933-53

Below When only about ten years old, Car 830, built in 1928 and painted in the lined-out prewar livery, takes the curve from the Horse Fair into Bristol Street on its way out of the city on the 36 route to Cotteridge. The width of the Horse Fair reflected its former use as an occasional market place, the last horse fair having been held here in 1911.

The buildings to the right of the tram in this *circa* 1938 view are still there today. The White Lion public house, with its clock tower, still does business on the corner of Thorp Street, especially with theatre-goers attending performances at the nearby Birmingham Hippodrome. All the buildings on the left, including St Catherine of Sienna Roman Catholic church, the nearby school and the two small thoroughfares of Windmill Street and Little Bow Street have all been swept away.

Car 830 would later become one of the most photographed of all Birmingham's trams, when, with open balcony four-wheeler car 367, it toured what was left of the Birmingham system on 10 July 1949. *D. R. Harvey collection*

Below left There has been very little change in the character of the Horse Fair between the previous pre-war picture and the early part of 1952, when similar Maley & Taunton air-brake car 815 is seen a few yards further on, travelling towards the city. It is about to pass some roadworks; this is an obvious hazard to other traffic, but it appears that the tram service is unaffected by the repairs. The temporary warning oil lamps can be seen between the tramcar and the Morris Oxford taxi that has just turned out of Essex Street. To the left of the tram is a 'Tramway Repairs Keep Left' sign, warning other traffic of the obstruction in the carriageway.

Car 815 worked on the 5½-mile Cotteridge route for almost all of its 24 years in service. During this time it amassed just over 700,000 miles. Its side panel carries an advertisement for Capstan cigarettes; tobacco advertising today is a controversial subject, but it was quite unusual for Birmingham tramcars to advertise cigarettes. In nearly 50 years of operation only three such advertisements were ever carried by Birmingham's trams; one for K4 cigarettes was carried in the 1930s (see page 15), while Martin's Gold Leaf and Capstans were advertised between 1951 and 1953.

The M&T cars represented the last of the traditional style of Birmingham tram. Although new rocker-panelled trams were, by 1928, becoming rather outmoded, beneath the surface these BCT tramcars represented some of the most up-to-date technology in air-brake design. They provided an independent air-wheel brake to all eight wheels as well as an air-track brake. This provided much smoother and more controllable braking compared with the previous EMB Class. These 16¾-ton tramcars were regarded as very 'sure footed' and provided the Cotteridge route with the most up-to-date trams in the Birmingham fleet. *R. T. Wilson*

Left The 'palm tree' advertisement on the wall above the shoe-repairers near the corner of Sun Street is something of a climatic non sequitur on this damp Saturday, 21 June 1952, just two weeks before the closure of the Cotteridge and Bristol Road routes. The traffic-light-controlled junction in Bristol Street, over which Short Brothers-bodied car 829 is passing, was the crossing point of the number 8 Inner Circle bus route. Most of Bristol Street was tree-lined and was a dignified, if somewhat run-down, approach from the south-west by the main A38 road into the city.

Today this junction does not exist. All the buildings in the background were swept away in the Lee Bank comprehensive redevelopment plan that affected the area immediately to the north-west of Bristol Street at the end of the 1950s. Not only were high-rise flats built upon the site of the shops, but Bristol Street itself was widened into a four-lane dual carriageway as part of the Middle Ring Road scheme of the 1970s, creating an underpass section linking the former Belgrave Road with Lee Bank. It would be very difficult to identify this location today. *J. Cull*

Right Cotteridge depot's normal allocation of tramcars consisted of all the 30 trams of the 812 Class together with the two lightweight trams, cars 842 and 843. The depot did, however, draw upon the allocation of Selly Oak depot for up to four or five extra trams from about 1950. The first type of air-brake car, the Brush-bodied EMB cars of the 732 Class, were favoured in these temporary transfers; they could easily be recognised as they were of four-bay construction. Cotteridge's regular allocation of the totally enclosed 812 Class had the eight-windowed upper saloon arrangement common to all the later standard air-brake bogie cars. A further distinguishing feature of the 732 Class, which car 750 clearly shows, was the fitting of the cleaners' balcony grab rails on the underside of the roof adjacent to the destination number blind. This particular tram was first used by Cotteridge depot by April 1950 and remained there until September of the following year, and therefore dates this view to within that 17-month period.

The tram is seen in Bristol Road approaching Speedwell Road at an architecturally interesting point in the housing development along this route. The housing up to Pebble Mill Road was generally Victorian or Edwardian, but this was the first point where inter-war infilling had taken place, as shown by the white-painted 1930s vintage house behind the post box. *C. Carter*

Below The major alterations that have affected Bristol Road have been at the major road junctions. Car 763 rumbles across the traffic lights at the Priory Road intersection with Bristol Road; the large house on the corner is Greenmore College, a private school. The tram is working the 36 route in the early spring of 1952, and is on its way out of the city, travelling towards Pebble Mill Road which will take it eventually to the terminus at Cotteridge. Car 763 was allocated to Cotteridge depot for just under two months from March 1952.

Approaching the city is one of Midland Red's BMMO D5B types, which were amongst the last double-decker buses to be bodied by Brush of Loughborough between 1950 and 1952, when the firm stopped body manufacturing. This type of vehicle remained in service until the mid-1960s, and just as Brush-built tram 763 belongs to the last generation of standard Birmingham tramcars, so the bus represents the last of the traditional heavyweight Midland Red double-deckers. *R. T. Wilson*

Below The first member of the 30-strong 732 Class turns into Pebble Mill Road from Bristol Road when working the 36 route to Cotteridge in June 1952. The condition of the track by this time had deteriorated from its pristine state of the inter-war years, as can be seen in the foreground. Only essential track repairs were undertaken once the decision to abandon the routes had been taken. Gradually the ride on the trams became more akin to an endurance test for the intrepid traveller who experienced a fast ride

out to Rednal or Rubery. On the more leisurely run out to Cotteridge, minor track deformities were of less importance than for instance on Bristol Road's reserved track.

These lower-numbered examples of the first class of air-brake cars purchased in 1926 had led reasonably quiet lives working mainly from Rosebery Street depot, where they were used on the fairly short 33 route to Ladywood. The day after Rosebery Street closed on Saturday 30 August 1947, the eleven 732 Class trams remaining there were moved to Selly Oak. Their excellent condition was soon put to the test on the high-speed Bristol Road routes, but they were used from time to time along Pershore Road to augment Cotteridge depot's fleet, as shown here. *R. Brook*

Middle left Cotteridge-based Short Brothers car 823 has just reached the junction with Bristol Road having come up the slight rise on the reserved track of Pebble Mill Road; it will turn right across the southbound carriageway of Bristol Road before reaching the passenger shelter and Bundy clocks, which were shared with the Rednal and Rubery tram routes. Today the large gabled house looks out over the deserted grassed-over central reservation, and very few visitors to the city would ever realise that this had ever been a busy tram junction.

The design details of these last traditional 812 Class Birmingham trams can be appreciated in this view. Their bodies continued the style of the previous 762 batch, in that the upper saloons were equipped with eight small windows between the bulkheads, enabling each row of passengers to control their own ventilation. Below the staircase at one end, beneath the lower saloon waistrail, are the ventilation louvres that were intended to prevent the rheostats from overheating; these are visible on the tram just to the right of the central reservation bollard, and were fitted to the complete class of 30 trams after 1937. Maley & Taunton provided the Burnley-style maximum traction bogies. These broke the pattern of the previous five orders, which had all gone to EMB of Eagle Works, Moor Street, West Bromwich. The M&T design could be distinguished by the slightly squarer-topped axle-boxes. *R. Brook*

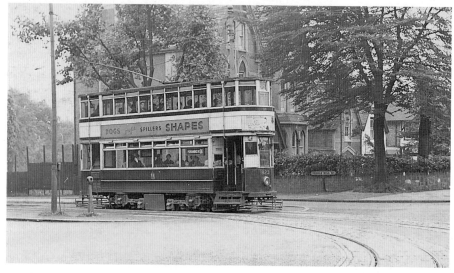

Bottom left Travelling in the opposite direction, towards Cotteridge, the Pershore Road trams turned left into Pebble Mill Road within a few hundred yards of gaining the reserved track in Bristol Road. Pebble Mill Road provided an access between Bristol Road and Pershore Road, and was used because Kings Norton UDC wished to gain access to the existing CBT lines on nearby Bristol Road and this was the shortest link between the two.

The Calthorpe family owned most of the land in the Edgbaston area and prohibited the building of anything to do with industry or commerce on it, although from about the 1860s they had to admit ordinary families on to their estate. The houses built for these better-paid artisans were confined to the eastern and northern parts nearest to the inner areas of Birmingham. For the remainder, some of the best-known industrialists associated with the growth of Birmingham, the Cadbury, Chamberlain, Martineau, Ryland and Sturge families, all lived on the Calthorpe Estate. As a direct consequence, the protectionist policy measures to ensure the dignity of the area affected something as mundane as ensuring that trees were planted and that services such as shops were kept to the minimum, and then only on the periphery of their land. Even the access of the tram routes through the 'well-heeled' estate became a point of issue.

The first section of dual carriageway in the city was built immediately prior to the First World War in Oxhill Road, Handsworth, but Pebble Mill Road was the first dual carriageway designed to accept trams running down the centre on a reserved, segregated track. It was opened in 1919 when it was described as a 'specimen road' and acted as a model for the main arterial routes such as Bristol Road, **Tyburn Road and Stratford Road.** *C. Carter*

Pebble Mill Road to Cotteridge

Top From Monday 3 September 1951 until the abandonment of the Bristol Road and Cotteridge routes on 5 July 1952, Pebble Mill Road was used for parking trams. This was because of the lack of space in Selly Oak depot while its ten roads of track were converted for bus operation. As a result two new cross-overs were built in August 1951 so that the inbound track could be used for parking trams. Up to about 20 trams could be accommodated on this line, which was protected at either end by traffic lights, activated by skates on the overhead. This was necessary as the outward-bound line was now effectively made into single-track for the length of Pebble Mill Road.

Car 828 leaves the single-line section, passing the tram signal light and the wooden hut used by the BCT watchman during the depot conversion period. On the inbound line is the usual line of parked Selly Oak trams, the one car visible being 782. A third overhead wire can be seen in this view; this was put in so that service cars on their own wires could pass the parked trams without the need for any de-poling. *R. Brook*

Middle Another closer view of the stabling operation shows Brush-bodied EMB air-brake car 788 at the rear of a row of tightly packed, parked Selly Oak-allocated trams. Only the fifth tram in the line belongs to one of the earlier classes, distinguishable by being the only one having four windows between the bulkheads and not the eight of the later 762 Class.

Behind the line of trams is the open land which for many years was occupied by a riding school. The abiding memory of this site is of a succession of grey horses that seemed fascinated by the passing traffic! Today the land is occupied by the BBC's Pebble Mill Studio complex and the roadway is usually lined with parked cars overflowing from its car park. *R. T. Wilson*

Bottom The distant Ford Anglia disappears along the trackless Pershore Road, alongside Cannon Hill Park, while tram 813 prepares to leave the reserved track on Pebble Mill Road and taken the right turn into Pershore Road. The layout of the overhead can be clearly seen in this view; the extra wires coming from near the top of the traction pole belong to the electrical feeders that feed current into the overhead at intervals along every route. The photographer, Ray Wilson, is standing on the River Rea bridge, which until 1911 was the boundary between Birmingham and Kings Norton.

The group of children, including a man carrying his young daughter, wait for a city-bound tram at the oblong, red compulsory tram stop, perhaps after a visit to Cannon Hill Park. The 80-acre park was another site donated to the town of Birmingham by Miss L. A. Ryland and was opened to the public on 1 September 1873. If the Lickey Hills at Rednal were the day-trippers' resort at the edge of the city, Cannon Hill Park was large enough to be a lung of green space within the city that would attract people looking for less arduous arboreal walks. The park was also served by the 37 tram route, which went to Willows Road via Balsall Heath. *R. T. Wilson*

PERSHORE RD. SELLY PARK

Top Car 791 was one of the 1928 vintage, Brush-built 762 Class EMB air-brake cars that had spent most of their operating life running from Washwood Heath depot equipped with a bow collector instead of a trolleypole. The tram is on the bridge over Bourn Brook, a small tributary stream which had its confluence with the River Rea in nearby Cannon Hill Park. It is seen on 3 June 1952 about halfway through its two-month allocation to Cotteridge, where it remained until the closure of that depot.

Car 791 seems in remarkably good condition, despite having little more than one month's service life left. Even at this late stage of its career the dark blue saloon paintwork is still good enough to reflect the fence of Cannon Hill Park in its varnished finish. *A. N. H. Glover*

Middle This *circa* 1916 view probably shows car 362, one of the 1912 UEC-built open-balcony trams that were mounted on UEC 7 ft 6 in trucks. It is passing First Avenue as it travels along Pershore Road in Selly Park. At that time these four-wheelers would have had only a few years left before being displaced by the 512 Class bogie trams, which would serve the Cotteridge route until they in turn were displaced by the arrival of the air-brake 812 cars of 1929.

The condition of the road surface in this early street scene is of interest. The Corporation Tramways Department was responsible for its tramlines and the adjacent 18 inches on either side of the tracks. For many years, until the 1930s, quite often the remainder of the road surface, as shown here, was of inferior quality. Therefore the stories of cars and bicycles getting their spindly tyres caught in the lines were quite often true, as the only reasonable road surface over which they could travel was on the properly maintained tram tracks. *Commercial postcard*

Bottom Car 839 approaches Kitchener Road while working the Selly Park section of Pershore Road on Saturday 5 July 1952. Normal services were maintained throughout this last day of operation and the only things that distinguished this Saturday from any other were the notices pasted on the upper saloon balcony windows and the tram stop temporarily affixed to one of the replacement bus stop posts.

The following day car 839 would be placed in store on the Bristol Road central reservation near Eastern Road; on Friday 11 July it would be driven across the city, along with seven others, to Witton depot where it would be broken up by W. T. Bird.

Views of trams on this section of Pershore Road are very uncommon. On this curve there was a 'tram pinch' traffic sign warning other road users that the tram tracks crossed to the east side of the carriageway for about 20 yards and took a different line from the curve of the road. The two tracks can be seen in the foreground some distance away from the nearside kerb.

The present-day urban landscape has hardly changed in the intervening decades, yet the whole ambience of this scene is redolent of another time, when public transport was a major facet of city life and the tramcar in Birmingham was the prime mover of people for work and leisure. *A. K. Terry*

Top The Dogpool Inn stood on the corner of Dogpool Lane and Pershore Road at Ten Acres. This garish self-advertising hostelry was the original public house at this crossroads, but despite all its immodest and boastful self-proclamation, it was demolished at the end of the 1920s and replaced by a Birmingham Municipal Bank. The pub on the opposite corner at St Stephens Road, the Ten Acres Tavern, was also pulled down. The replacement licensed premises for both was built on the site of the Ten Acres Tavern but was confusingly named the Dogpool! It is now know as The Hibernian.

The tramcar appears to be either car 323 or 353; these belonged to the 301 Class of four-wheel UEC open-balcony cars that replaced the ex-CBT trams on the Cotteridge route. It is seen in about 1913 at approximately the same position as the 1951 view of car 816 below, and displays the flop-over destination boards that were used on Birmingham tramcars from 1909 until about 1920 when they were replaced by the more familiar small, square route number boxes. It is also carrying an advertisement proclaiming that the Great Western Railway has the shortest route to London. This would also date the photograph in the years immediately prior to the First World War as the GWR opened its Bicester 'cut-off' line through Aynho for passenger services between Birmingham Snow Hill and London on 1 July 1910. *D. R. Harvey collection*

Middle The first member of the Short Brothers class of 1928 stands at the Ten Acres junction with Dogpool Lane on its way to Cotteridge. It is opposite Selly Park school with the tall nave of Selly Park Baptist church visible above the tramcar.

There appears to be a delay, because the man standing in the roadway adjacent to the entrance to the tram seems to be in conversation with the couple on the pavement. A photograph is a one-twenty-fifth-of-a-second moment in time, so what happened next must be open to conjecture. One hopes that the Austin 10 that is approaching the tram stopped, or the man made his mind up and got aboard the 36 service tram.

This 1952 view shows the extent of the straight run that the cars made from the distant bend at Kitchener Road, past the long row of terraced houses on the right. These were always known as the ABC houses, each being named in alphabetical order after places in the British Isles. This ambitious building programme stopped at the letter 'J' for Jarrow - the rest of the alphabet was never built! *R. Brook*

Bottom The horse-drawn delivery van crosses Pershore Road and trots into Dogpool lane opposite Ten Acres Post Office one summer's day in 1952. The early post-war MG Magnette four-door saloon is parked on the wrong side of the road outside Adams's tobacconists and confectionery shop as the shadow cast by the 16³/₄-ton tramcar passes across it.

This section of the Pershore Road route marked the change from the large Victorian/Edwardian terraced housing of Selly Park to the mid-19th-century mixed residential and industrial land use associated with the Ten Acres area of Stirchley. The settlement of Ten Acres grew up around the nearby Dogpool Mill, which as well as being an iron-forge, was also at the site of the crossing point of the River Rea. The wide former turnpike route of Pershore Road narrowed at this point because of this small hamlet, and the tram tracks were reduced to a single line from this junction to Cartland Road. Car 816 waits for the approaching city-bound tramcar to leave the single line before itself negotiating the narrow quarter-mile section with its one passing loop. *Lens of Sutton*

Below The strangely shaped towers of the Dogpool public house stand out on the skyline above car 828 in the spring of 1952 as it passes towards the end of the Dogpool single-line section of track. This tram, one of the Maley & Taunton air-brake cars constructed by Short Brothers in 1928, is on its way to the city terminus in Navigation Street, some three and a half miles away. It is approaching the out of city turnback point of the 53 route, which was a short-working of the main 36 service. The northern end of the passing loop is just to the right of the tram, near the Mitchells & Butlers advertisement for its 'Export' brand of bottled light ale. The Dogpool passing loop was used by trams going to Cotteridge in order that city-bound trams could clear the next narrow section of line. *R. Brook*

Middle This part of Pershore Road is still a bottle-neck today, and the scene in August 1993 has hardly changed at all. The main difference is that a number of the mid-19th-century houses were demolished in the 1980s and an access road was built to serve a small trading estate on the land to the right of the large advertisement. The condition of the houses on the left and the taller buildings behind the advertisement hoarding suggest that they also may not last much longer. At least one of the Victorian terraces is boarded-up and a succession of fires in the buildings opposite the Ansells public house have left a number of these premises derelict for a number of years. In recent years the Dogpool public house has been renamed The Hibernian in an attempt to give the premises a more marketable image.

West Midlands Travel MCW Metrobus Mk I 2184 (GOC 184W) is passing the site of the tramway passing loop, which can still be identified by the short section of widened carriageway to the right. The bus is working on the 47 route, a service that was introduced on 2 April 1967 into the Groveley Lane part of Cofton. *D. R. Harvey*

Bottom The 29 cars of the 812-841 Class that survived the Second World War were all repainted into the post-war standard livery between September 1946 and September 1949. Car 817, working the 36 route and seen on the Dogpool loop from the other side of the road in about 1948, is still adorned in the pre-war arrangement of the livery with cream rocker-panels, lined-out paintwork and ornate-style fleet numbers. Car 817 was the penultimate member of the class to receive the post-war livery in March 1949, with only car 839 surviving longer in the old style of paintwork.

Tram 817 was one of 25 members of the 812-841 Class to be reseated with 'in-line' instead of staggered upholstered tilting seats in the last four years before the outbreak of the Second World War. As a result its seating capacity of 27 passengers in the lower saloon and 33 in the upper was reduced by two from its original seating capacity. Tram 817 was also one of the first four of the class to be experimentally fitted with external louvred panels in the dash panels to overcome the constant problem of heating rheostats. This modification was done in the spring of 1937 and, as a consequence of its success, the remainder of the class were similarly modified. Car 817 did not quite see out its full life span as it was withdrawn in late May 1952 because of loose tyres which, at that late stage, were not considered replacing. It was sent to Witton depot and was among the first cars after the Bristol/Pershore Road abandonment to be broken up by W. T. Bird & Son early in July 1952. *R. Herbert*

Top Car 839 approaches Stirchley having left behind the distant towers of the Dogpool public house. This end of the single-line Dogpool section was characterised on the eastern side by rows of small cottage-style terraced Victorian housing dating from the 1860s. These opened straight on to the pavement and their proximity to the noisy passage of the trams in the narrow roadway may have been a source of great irritation to their occupants.

Later Victorian town planning attempted to avoid, where possible, the mistakes of earlier generations in that residential areas were segregated from industrial ones. Here in Stirchley the development of small industrial premises opposite the housing was a consequence of the industrial growth of the late 18th and early 19th centuries. This generally occurred where small streams were crossed by main routeways, in this case Griffins Brook which flowed into the nearby River Rea, and the water supply was harnessed by water mills to provide power. The small enclave of metal-based industries opposite the houses in the Ten Acres area along Pershore Road was an early-20th-century relocation of the previous industrial sites that included Dogpool Mill, which was an iron rolling mill. The juxtaposition of housing and industry produced an area that always looked in need of renovation; it is surprising, therefore, that most of the buildings seen here in 1952 still remain occupied. *R. Brook*

Middle Beyond the Warwards Lane junction with Pershore Road lay the bridge over Griffins Brook and the adjacent Cartland Road. On the corner was the Pavilion Cinema, opened on 28 November 1931 and standing out both architecturally and culturally as a product of the 1930s. Its gaunt, white-pillared frontage can be seen to the right of car 823.

This 63 hp tram, powered by two English Electric DK30/1L motors and mounted on Maley & Taunton Burnley maximum traction bogies, entered service in late 1928 and spent all of its working life giving trouble-free service to the residents along the Pershore Road route. At least one member of the 812 Class only ever visited Kyotts Lake Road Works for repainting and normal overhaul and never needed anything other than routine maintenance.

Car 823 is in the 1946 livery style, but has yet to receive the simpler style of fleet number that was applied after 1948. As yet devoid of advertisements, it would soon receive them for Spillers Shapes dog biscuits and Tide washingpowder. It is travelling towards the city and is about to enter the narrow single-line section of track leading to the Dogpool. *R. Herbert*

Bottom The approaching Short Brothers tramcar, 839, is about to enter the one-way system in Stirchley. Southbound trams took the line to the right into Pershore Road while those going to the city terminus emerged from the track on the left from Hazelwell Street. The tram approaches the Three Horseshoes public houses which stands on the corner of Umberslade Road. Opposite, a 1934 Birmingham-registered Morris Ten is parked outside Dewhurst's butchers shop. The disappearing Midland Red doubledecker working the 147 route from Redditch is a Brush-bodied BMMO D5B, which entered service in 1951. This view of Stirchley, taken on 7 June 1952, shows another section of the Cotteridge route that has hardly altered in the intervening years. *H. B. Priestley*

Left At the tram stop in Bristol Road at Pebble Mill junction two cars cross on their way to their respective termini on a sunny day in 1949. Passengers hurriedly leave the city-bound car on the 70 route, while the driver of car 558, dressed in his summer uniform, clocks in at the Bundy clock. This tram is also working on the 70 route but is travelling towards Rednal. Both trams display the 1946 livery and although 558 had its fleet number repainted in the simpler post-1948 style, car 756 retained its shaded numerals until withdrawal in 1952. *C. Carter*

Middle At the wide open space of the Rubery terminus car 737, carrying the 'Beer at Home Means Davenports' advertisement, stands behind the unadorned 532, one of the 70 hp strengthened tramcars. Both are on the from-city track and have yet to move off into the single stub in order to reverse adjacent to where the large wrought iron and glass passenger shelter stood.

This 1949 view shows the subtle differences between the standard 1926 style of body on the newer air-brake car and the earlier former open-balconied, heavily rebuilt car 532. One easy point of identification for all the 732 Class was the small grab rail above both the side balcony windows just below the roof. This was to assist cleaners and depot maintenance staff to gain access to the roof of the tram. *C. Carter*

Below Brush-bodied air-brake bogie car 744 has just arrived at the Rednal terminus on Sunday 15 June 1952. The normal operation of tramcars to Rednal would not use the terminal loop but would run alongside the toilet block, just off the photograph to the left, and reverse in the single track, before returning to the city via Lickey Road. Tram 765 is parked on the loop and is being stabled there along with up to 14 others. This was the normal practice in the last month of operation as Selly Oak depot's capacity was much reduced by the conversion work necessary for bus operation. *R. Brook*

Right On the same day as the previous photograph, Brush-bodied eight-windowed car 779 leads four other cars stabled along the back part of the loop at Rednal terminus, with their trolleypoles down. They would return to service when the need arose and crews would be sent up from Selly Oak depot, some five miles away, to put the parked trams back in service.

The former Washwood Heath bow-collector tramcars can easily be distinguished in this view, as they have the eight windows between the upper saloon bulkheads. *R. Brook*

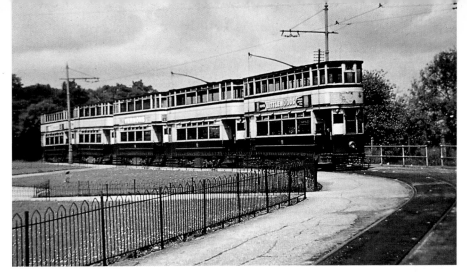

Middle Short Brothers-bodied Maley & Taunton bogie car 825 passes the row of shops at the corner of Pershore Road and Third Avenue in this rare 1952 colour shot. The tram is approaching the Selly Park Tavern, the tall building beyond the shops, on its way towards the city on the 36 route, and will shortly turn left into Pebble Mill Road.

In the foreground is the red-painted emergency fire-alarm box standing in front of the grassy bank that separated Upland Road from Oakfield Road, whose houses can be seen on the extreme left. This grassy area surprisingly remains today. *J. S. Webb*

Below In the lined-out prewar livery, four-wheeled car 420, one of the 50-strong 401 Class built in 1912 by UEC, stands at the tram stop at the Digbeth-Meriden Street junction, just beyond the elaborately styled Digbeth police station. It is working the 42 route to Alcester Lanes End and after passing the semi-circular, gable-fronted garage beyond the Morris Eight car, the tram will turn right into Rea Street before eventually gaining the main Moseley Road route.

Car 420 received its last repaint in September 1945 and was withdrawn on 1 October 1949 not long after this picture was taken. *C. Carter*

Top On the last day of operation, Saturday 5 July 1952, car 816 works its way beyond Stirchley Baths, built in 1911, and on towards the large out-of-town Ten Acres and Stirchley Co-operative Society store, the headquarters of the society. The building was demolished in the mid-1970s and was replaced by a large Co-op supermarket.

The houses and cottages, the latter dating from the 1840s, have long since disappeared to be replaced by discount warehouses, but the houses on the right and the one-way system in Hazelwell Street still remain.

The tram clearly shows the small Sanders rear lamp to the right of the headlight; this replaced the temporary rear light fitted for the blackout conditions which was mounted in a small box-like structure just above the fender. It at least gave motorists at night some indication as to where the rear of the tram was located in relation to the front of their car! Car 816 would continue to work normally throughout the rest of the Saturday, but the following morning would find it parked on the Bristol Road reservation which was a prelude to its imminent scrapping at Witton depot a few weeks later. *A. K. Terry*

Middle Beyond the southern bifurcation of Hazelwell Street and Pershore Road was a quarter-mile length of narrow street. This was the 1890s shopping development of Stirchley. The greengrocer in his white coat and apron puts out more produce as car 830 approaches the stop beneath the Church of the Ascension; this impressive brick and stone building with its castellated tower was built in the early years of this century, but gutted by fire in the early 1970s. It stood opposite the British Oak public house, also at the end of the one-way system, but this time in Pershore Road. British Oak was the second tram short-working along Pershore Road, and was numbered 46; it was a useful turn-back point and the reverse cross-over line visible in the foreground was put in to allow trams to turn back to work back into the city.

It is Saturday 7 June 1952 and car 830 is by now looking a little less presentable than when it was used for the tour of the system by the LRTL in July 1949. Within two months the tram would be broken up at Witton depot. *J. H. Meredith*

Bottom A similar, but much earlier, view of Stirchley. Photographs like this are always difficult to date - the style of the women's dresses and hats, the knickerbockered boys standing on the corner of Mary Vale Road and the fact that the general appearance of the clothing suggests an Edwardian summer, dates this view from about the year of the opening of the line in 1904 to about 1906.

Stirchley only really grew after the opening of the Birmingham and Western Suburban railway line on 3 April 1876, and then as an overspill area from the nearby Cadbury-owned garden suburb of Bournville. Cadbury Brothers opened the first part of their famous chocolate factory in September 1879, and in the nearby hamlet of Stirchley Street a lot of quite desirable, but less well-planned, speculative Victorian development took place. On Pershore Road the main shopping area was developed in the 1890s so that by the time the CBT opened its line to Cotteridge the buildings were still comparatively new. The approaching CBT car, which appears to be either 163 or 168, is travelling towards Cotteridge on the single-line track passing through the by now busy shopping suburb. *D. R. Harvey collection*

Top When the Pershore Road service was introduced by CBT on 20 May 1904 a temporary terminus just short of Fordhouse Lane was used; presumably the last section of tracks was not yet ready for use. The line was extended to Cotteridge on 23 June 1904. Car 242, later to become Birmingham Corporation 472, stands opposite Elmtree Road at the entrance to the last passing loop on the newly opened line. Just visible on the destination box is the destination paper sticker that shows the route to be STIRCHLEY & BREEDON CROSS, so the photograph must have been taken between the above two dates. To the right of the view is the small chapel that stood on the corner of Mayfield Road. *Commercial postcard*

Middle On a wet and miserable 27 December 1951, car 837 loads its wet passengers *en route* for Cotteridge at the far end of Stirchley near to the Fordhouse Lane junction. Behind the approaching Morris Ten car is the rise over the Worcester & Birmingham Canal and the Midland Railway freight loop line.

The advertisements on the hoardings advertise products such as Lucas car batteries, the long-forgotten Nosegay cigarettes and St Martin's Chunky Marmalade, whose product was displayed prominently on a large number of Birmingham trams after 1951. What is amusing, with today's more health-conscious life-style, is the juxtaposition of the advertisements for Bass Red Triangle beer with that for Aspro headache-relieving tablets!

Car 837 was the only member of the 812-841 Class to be repainted in the wartime all-over grey livery in January 1942, being returned to the standard simplified post-war livery in October 1946. *R. J. S. Wiseman*

Bottom Looking down the hill in the opposite direction, car 836 has just left the compulsory stop beside the advertisement hoardings and is passing the newsagent's shop at the corner of Fordhouse Lane where car 821 turned over during the Second World War. The view from Breedon bridge towards the city shows the nature of Pershore Road looking into the Stirchley Street section of the tram route. The narrow Victorian shopping area disappears towards the one-way street system at Hazelwell Street about half a mile away. The view reveals, even in the relatively traffic-free early 1950s, large numbers of parked vehicles beside the tramway. The impending growth in the numbers of private cars over the next few years would increase congestion dramatically in the late-19th-century suburbs. The tramcar, already regarded as a slow, tall, gaunt and space-consuming vehicle, was seen as an anachronism that added to the congestion, especially as kerb-side loading was rarely used in Birmingham. Until parking restrictions became the norm, trams would be impeded by stationary and manoeuvring vehicles encroaching on to the tram tracks. The anti-tram lobby used this as an argument against the tramcar, but interestingly the same criticism could be made about the buses of today, as parked vehicles often prevent them from reaching the kerb. *F. N. Lloyd Jones*

Stirchley

Top Brush-built EMB air-brake car 732 comes slowly down Breedon bridge at Lifford on 15 June 1952, having stopped at the compulsory stop at the top of the bridge opposite the Breedon Cross public house in the background behind the tram. It was here that Maley & Taunton air-brake car 821 overturned on 26 October 1942. It was left unattended at the Cotteridge terminus without the handbrake being properly applied; the air brake leaked off and the tram just rolled away from the terminus, finally coming to grief at the bottom of the bridge at Fordhouse Lane when its top deck was ripped off after it left the rails and turned over.

Like many of its Class, car 732 had led a fairly nomadic career since its construction in September 1926, having been at Rosebery Street, Washwood Heath and Selly Oak depots before spending its second spell at Cotteridge in the last two months of operation in 1952. *J. H. Price*

Middle The Breedon Cross pub was just beyond the bridge. Opposite, to the right of the tram, was the Savoy cinema. This closed on 2 February 1958 with the showing of the film *Women's Prison*.

Car 838 has crested the bridge and will follow the Midland Red D5B up the Victorian terrace-lined hill towards Cotteridge terminus. It is Monday 30 June 1952 and the car already carries in its balcony windows the dreaded notices to warn passengers that the route will shortly be abandoned and replaced by buses.

The late Victorian/Edwardian growth of housing around the Breedon Cross was associated with the local industry that grew up around the nearby Worcester & Birmingham Canal and the Midland Railway's lines. Industrial sites such as the Kings Norton Metal Company, which made coinage strip and blanks in copper bronze, were attracted by the advantages of cheap transport. In later years Lifford Lane led to Kings Norton factory centre, although the access was limited by the low height of the railway bridge over that road. *F. N. Lloyd Jones*

Bottom Once the Breedon Cross bridge was crossed, Pershore Road continued to rise steeply until the ridge from which Cotteridge took its name was reached. Immediately beyond the flatter section of the route that was reached at Francis Road, the road crossed two railway lines, the first being the Lifford Curve linking the former Midland Railway route via Moseley and Camp Hill into Birmingham with the later 1876 Birmingham and Western Suburban line. The latter left Kings Norton station and followed the line of the Birmingham & Worcester Canal via Bournville and Selly Oak to Edgbaston before plunging through the tunnel into New Street Station in the city centre.

Car 823 is crossing this second bridge between Holly Road, which the Leyland Comet lorry has just passed, and Midland Road, which lies out of the picture to the left of the only city-bound motorcar in the photograph. The tram has just gone beyond the Grant Arms tram stop at Ivy Road, which was the last stop before the terminus. The bus stop in the foreground, which would serve the replacement 45 bus route, was already in use for the Outer Circle bus service that traversed Pershore Road between Fordhouse Land and Cotteridge. This is the last day of tram operation along Pershore Road and on the following day, Sunday 6 July 1952, a succession of Daimler CVG6s and Guy Arab IVs would operate the route. *A. K. Terry*

54   BIRMINGHAM TRAMS 1933-53

Above The last member of the 812 Class of Maley & Taunton air-brake bogie cars leaves Cotteridge on 6 November 1951 and passes the shops just before the junction with Midland Road. One of these shops, Wallace & Co is advertising that they are Bush dealers; they are using the expression wireless rather than the later word radio, yet are selling the latest televisions which, in 1951, were only recently becoming available on the mass market. Shops like this would have taken advantage of the fact that the BBC had opened its Sutton Coldfield transmitter two years earlier on Saturday 17 December 1954, making television reception available in the West Midlands area.

The tram will continue down the slight descent from the Cotteridge terminus over the railway bridge, the wall of which is surmounted by the distant advertising hoardings. It would then pass the Grant Arms public house, whose large wooden sign can just be discerned against the gable end of the farthest row of late-19th-century shops. *R. B. Parr*

Right Although seen earlier in Pebble Mill Road, this excellent close-up view of car 843 affords the opportunity to look at the salient design features of this, Birmingham's last tram, in more detail.

The lightweight Brush-built car entered service in September 1930. In the space of two years the Bolton Road and Hagley Road abandonments had taken place and the era of up-to-date AEC Regent 661 buses with a variety of piano-front bodies had arrived. Their large-scale introduction effectively brought to a halt any further thoughts of tramway development in the city.

Car 843 was one of the first tramcars built in this country to belong to the interesting transitional designs that developed into the more streamlined double-deckers of the mid to late 1930s. The roughly contemporary Liverpool Cabin bogie cars, LUT No 1 and the Leeds 'Horsfield' trams had a less traditional appearance than their predecessors, but perhaps were not as modern in their design as Blackpool Corporation's 'Balloons', Belfast's 'McCreary' cars, Edinburgh's post-1933 four-wheelers, Glasgow's 'Coronation' cars and Liverpool's 'Green Goddesses'. Birmingham's

last tram still looked vaguely like the earlier Birmingham bogie car and retained the normal standard fixtures and fittings, and even a waistrail. It did, however, have a domed roof, and even if the plethora of upper-saloon side windows gave a fussy appearance, the lower saloon windows, ventilation system and destination boxes built in to the side panels gave the impression of a fairly radical move towards modernity.

The tram was built because of the mutual interest of the Brush Electrical Company and Birmingham's management team in the development of lightweight tramcar construction. It is therefore not altogether surprising that the end result resembled a standard Birmingham tramcar and a much smaller version of the cars that Brush had built for the Swansea & Mumbles system in 1928. The car was fitted with two GEC WT28AS 40 hp motors and weighed only 12 tons 6 cwt 1 qt, which was 4 tons 9 cwt less than a standard Birmingham tram. Always allocated to Cotteridge depot, it is seen in company with car 837 at Cotteridge in 1947. *A. D. Packer*

Cotteridge terminus

Below The Edwardian shopping centre at Cotteridge was reached by the electric trams of the City of Birmingham Tramways Co Ltd on 23 June 1904, Kings Norton and Northfield UDC having obtained the powers to construct the line in 1901. The large imposing tower of the then recently completed St Agnes's Church (demolished in 1986) is visible above the 11 gable-ended shops as CBT car 242 waits at the terminal stub just beyond the depot entrance line. This entrance ran alongside the newly constructed shops to the right of the tram.

This photograph was almost certainly taken in the summer of 1904 as another commercial postcard of the same tram at the temporary Stirchley terminus in May 1904 seems to have some of the same small boys in it.

Car 242 was one of the 239-242 Class that were built to a Brush design at Kyotts Lake Road Works in 1904, being among the first of CBT's 'Aston' type. They were small tramcars, being only 27 ft 6 in long, mounted on Brush AA 6 ft 6 in trucks with two 25 hp Brush 1002D motors and a seating capacity of 48. Tram 242 was taken into BCT stock in January 1912 in CBT's green livery as car 472 after having been transferred from Bournbrook depot to Witton by 1907 and subsequently re-equipped with a Brush 8-foot wheelbase truck. In 1924 it was top-covered, vestibuled and re-equipped with Dick, Kerr 6A 35 hp motors. This extended the tram's working life until June 1938 when it was withdrawn and broken up at West Smethwick depot in August of that year. *Commercial postcard*

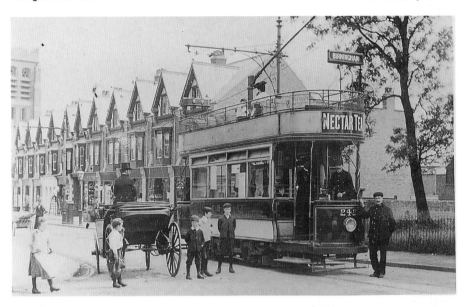

Middle Some 47 years later, car 833 leaves the Cotteridge shopping area on 5 April 1951, while the first member of the class, car 812, waits to move up to the terminus.

Cotteridge remained the terminus of the Pershore Road route throughout its 48 years of operation. Although extensions were tentatively proposed towards Kings Norton, nothing came of these plans and further extensions to Kings Norton and West Heath were subsequently undertaken by buses. In the foreground the cloth-capped man walks across the depot entrance lines as a motor cyclist, riding without a crash helmet, passes the depot entrance.

The A441 Pershore Road was the main arterial route between Birmingham and Redditch, and the Cotteridge suburban shopping centre was the last commercial area within the city boundary along this route. As a consequence there was usually a number of parked cars and delivery vehicles adding to the congestion. As well as the Ford Anglia saloon, there is an Austin A40 10 cwt van, a Morris-Commercial Equiload delivery van and, beyond the roller-shuttered light commercial on the nearside kerb, is a Standard Vanguard van, travelling towards the city. *H. B. Priestley*

Bottom In this third view of the 36 route terminus, experimental lightweight car 842 stands on the stub in 1952, in company with car 822. Compared with the 1904 view above, St Agnes's Church and the row of 11 shops still remain but the open space beyond the depot entrance has been filled by the stone-faced Barclays Bank, standing behind the utility bus shelters for the Outer Circle bus route. Originally there were two curves into the depot so that trams could turn towards the city or to the single parking line, which extended about 30 yards to a position opposite Watford Road. By 1952 only the southern curve remained, which meant that all cars leaving or returning to the depot had to be re-poled after a reversing operation.

Car 842 is one of the two lightweight cars allocated to Cotteridge depot, but as we have seen it is doubtful whether either was going to become the precursor of a new fleet of tramcars. However, they did signal the way the Transport Department was thinking in terms of a modern tram design. By the time this photograph was taken, the all-metal Short Brothers tram had been mounted on the Maley & Taunton bogies from the runaway tram, 821, which altered it from being the lowest in the fleet to the highest bogie car remaining in service after 1950. This gave this splendid-looking tram a rather perched look, atop newly fitted **bogies**. *D. R. Harvey collection*

Top Another trio of views of the terminus. The Cotteridge area of Kings Norton UDC was still relatively new when CBT car 202, painted in the Munich Lake and Cream livery, was photographed at the terminus in about 1905. This 48-seat open-topped tram had been built by Brush in 1904 and operated for much of its CBT life from Witton. It had previously been thought that after being allocated for its first four months of service to Bournbrook depot, which would also include Cotteridge depot as it was regarded as an outlying sub-depot, car 202 was transferred to Witton depot, the northern operational base for CBT opened on 1 October 1904. Yet here it is in Cotteridge carrying two advertisements for shops on the south side of Birmingham. The advert on the rocker panel is for H. Faulkes, Family Grocer, whose premises are behind the tram on the corner of Watford Road.

After being transferred to the Corporation fleet on 1 January 1912, CBT 202 became car 462. This 'Aston'-type car was eventually top-covered in 1924 and was finally withdrawn in May 1938.

Over the next two photographs one can see how little Cotteridge has changed in 90 years. One thing that did alter remarkably quickly was the removal of the walls in front of the houses beyond the tram in Pershore Road as these buildings became retail premises at about the time of the First World War. *Lens of Sutton*

Middle On a sunny Spring morning in 1951 car 836 waits in the single line opposite the entrance to Cotteridge depot before the driver clocks in at the Bundy clock and starts off on the five-mile run to the city terminus at Navigation Street. These Maley & Taunton-bogied, Short Brothers-bodied cars of 1928 were regarded by the motormen as being the best of all the 63 hp air-brake trams. Although they were not usually able to produce sparkling performances on the Pershore Road route, they were reliable and comfortable vehicles.

One of the earlier Brush-built EMB cars, 758, waits opposite the row of shops which were situated on the west side of Pershore Road. It will move up to the terminus stop once the eight-windowed 836 starts its city-bound journey. It has just been passed by a Midland Red SOS FEDD (Front Entrance Double-Decker), which is working on the 147 route from Redditch. It is still painted in the pre-spray-painted style of livery; this was replaced by an all-over red colour scheme, causing the silver roof and lining to be lost. *G. W. Morant*

Bottom The present-day scene in Cotteridge is not much altered. The buildings in the background date from the decade before the turn of the century, yet the first floor upwards they have retained their characteristic bay windows, while the last 11 in the block were built with attic lights.

In August 1993 Alexander H45/31F-bodied Scania N113DR 3217 (H217 LOM) accelerates away from the mini-traffic island at Watford Road in company with the usual heavy traffic. It is passing the site of the depot entrance, just visible in the foreground. These buses, with their vivid acceleration and squealing brakes, certainly provide a service, in terms of speed and comfort, that the 812 Class trams could never do, although it is doubtful if they will live out a life of 24 years as did their illustrious predecessors. *D. R. Harvey*

Top The entrance to Cotteridge depot was sandwiched between a ladies' and gentlemen's public lavatory, appropriately segregated one on each side of the entrance, and can be seen behind the 1936 Morris Eight to the right of the telephone box; the Bundy clock used for registering departure times at the terminus can also be seen. The trams passed through this narrow entrance on a single line into the depot yard.

Cotteridge depot was closed for bus operation on 25 October 1986. When it was first opened by the City of Birmingham Tramways Company in June 1904, it was little more than a sub-depot to Bournbrook, with a capacity for only eight trams. It was subsequently taken over by BCT and extended in 1920-1 at a cost of £16,439 to its maximum capacity of 33 tram-cars.

Brush-built car 811, the last of the 40 EMB air-brake cars of 1928, has just moved off the single-line stub for its return trip to Birmingham. The car was transferred from Selly Oak on 15 May 1952 and would see out the last six weeks of its service life from Cotteridge. *R. Brook*

Middle Cotteridge depot yard opened out into a fan of eight tracks which, although giving a somewhat cramped area, was generally sufficient to cope with the needs of the 36 route cars. On the occasion of an enthusiasts' tour on 17 June 1951, cars 836, 842 and 837 stand in the depot, with the lightweight car having been used as the tour vehicle. Compared with earlier views, it can be seen that 842 sits higher on the track, and as a point of identification the shape of the valance between the bogies is much more rectangular than after its rebuild with the bogies from car 821. It is perhaps difficult to see the difference in height between the standard Birmingham tramcar and the experimental tram, but 842 was only 15 ft 3 in to the top of the trolleybase, although its more modern body shape gave the impression of being even lower. *D. R. Harvey collection*

Bottom For the tram enthusiast, the sight of a depot in the throes of being prepared for its conversion to bus operation was always a depressing one. This process was usually undertaken in the months prior to the change-over, and consisted of the tram pits being filled in and new bus maintenance pits being constructed. During the spring of 1952 the bulldozer and cement mixers moved in to Cotteridge depot, as they had done in the nearby Selly Oak depot some months earlier, and began the work that was the prelude to the abandonment.

The trams, doomed and soon to be made redundant, were regarded as time-expired, expendable commodities. Repairs on them were reduced to a minimum, which resulted in three of Cotteridge's tramcars being withdrawn early rather than spend unnecessary money on repairing what, in previous years, would have been regarded as fairly trivial items.

Looking for all the world like condemned prisoners, cars 748, the ubiquitous 842 and 816 stand between the conversion work and the entrance. Although they have a few months of work in front of them, the end of their service careers is in sight and the steady, slow run-down of this penultimate south-western part of the Birmingham tram system. *D. R. Harvey collection*

BIRMINGHAM TRAMS 1933-53

MOSELEY ROAD ROUTES

THE Moseley Road and Alcester Road services were a complicated inheritance for Birmingham Corporation from the City of Birmingham Tramways Company on the expiry of the former's steam tram leases on 31 December 1906. There were two basic groups of routes, those starting in the Hill Street/Navigation Street area, which corresponded with the former CBT steam services, and the later routes that began from the High Street area. Each of these groups of routes had various short-workings and those from the Hill Street termini are shown in the maps overleaf.

Hill Street/Navigation Street services

The original steam tram service to Moseley was opened by Birmingham Central Tramways on 28 December 1884, from Moat Row via Bradford Street and Moseley Road. This was extended on 20 June 1885 via Bromsgrove Street, Station Street and the newly opened John Bright Street to the terminus in Hill Street. It later served as the basis of the High Street routes.

The second route to open was that through Balsall Heath, which began operation on 19 July 1886 to join the main Moseley Road route about half a mile north of the terminus at St Mary's Row. The final mile to the Kings Heath terminus near to the Kings Heath depot at Silver Street was opened on 1 February 1887.

On the expiry of the CBT lease on 31 December 1906 it was transferred to the Corporation, which began operation with electric top-covered Radial cars of the 71 Class.

There were three main routes that began around the corner site near New Street Station's Queens Drive: **1**, the long Alcester Lanes End route via Balsall Heath, later to be numbered 39, which started in Hill Street; **2**, the Cannon Hill branch service to Willows Road, Edgbaston, which in the 1915 route numbering system became the 37; originally it had its terminus in Navigation Street at the Queens Hotel end, but in May 1944 exchanged its starting point with **3**, the Leopold Street and Highgate 41 route and went into Hill Street.

The three routes left the side of New Street Station and travelled past Station Street, which was the terminus for the Coventry Road and Stratford Road tram services. After crossing Smallbrook Street the trams passed the Empire and Hippodrome theatres and continued along Hurst Street, with its rather run-down Victorian shops and nearby market warehouses. The tracks into Bromsgrove Street were retained after the closure of the Stratford Road group of tram routes in January 1937, to enable Selly Oak, Cotteridge and Rosebery Street cars to reach Kyotts Lake Road Works. At the Sherlock Street junction the routes diverged.

Leopold Street

Crossing Sherlock Street, the outward-bound trams on the Leopold Street routes continued along a short section of Hurst Street before turning right into Bishop Street and, less than 100 yards later, turning left into MacDonald Street where they met the inbound track. Trams from Leopold Street going to the city continued to the MacDonald Street-Sherlock Street junction before turning right and then left into Hurst Street. The map overleaf shows the details.

This was an area of back-to-back and three-storeyed housing of the worst sort; decaying unsanitary houses were mixed with industrial premises, yet out of this unpromising mixture came a sense of community that subsequent urban renewal schemes failed to reproduce.

From MacDonald Street the tram route turned into Thomas Street and then into Leopold Street. The appalling inner city Victorian houses here were demolished in one of Birmingham's few pre-war housing redevelopment schemes at St Martin's Flats, which was completed in 1939. Between the wars Birmingham built an unprecedented 50,000 new houses, but these were mainly on the large outer municipal housing estates, many of which would never see a tram service.

Once past the flats the trams climbed the steep 1 in 13 hill in Leopold Street, passing the usual mixture of old housing and factories, before cresting the hill and taking the tight curve into Moseley Road. Here the trams ran amongst the Moseley Road cars, usually only as far as Trafalgar Road and the adjacent tram depot, although a few peak hour runs did go to Moseley, Kings Heath and Alcester Lanes End.

The steep gradient of Leopold Street meant that extra care had to be taken, especially when descending the hill.

The 401 Class, delivered from UEC in 1912-13 and fitted with Mountain & Gibson 7 ft 6 in trucks, were after several months fitted with the Spencer-Dawson air and oil brake, which failed in the 'on' position. These 50 trams ran for the rest of their working lives on the routes operated by Moseley Road depot, although the newer 702 Class operated on Sundays on the Leopold Street route until 1939.

Balsall Heath and Cannon Hill

The outward route of the route 37 and 39 Balsall Heath and Cannon Hill trams turned right from Hurst Street into Sherlock Street. Leaving behind the inbound line at Gooch Street, the route turned left into St Lukes Road and into an area of early Victorian detached housing, which had seen far better days.

St Lukes Road curved through a long right turn to cross Belgrave Road and the Inner Circle No 8 bus route. The trams then continued along Alexandra Road, with its late-19th-century terraced, bay-windowed houses before turning left into Balsall Heath Road. The cars stopped outside the Balsall Heath Picture House, which was the start of Balsall Heath's shopping area; they then immediately turned to the right into Clevedon Road and away from the shops.

City-bound trams crossed Balsall Heath Road a little further beyond the turn, so cars travelling in the opposite direction could, at this point, be seen scurrying from Cox Street West into the shop-lined Longmore Street. This part of the Balsall Heath system was characterised by the movement of trams following meandering courses, turning this way and that, in a maze of narrow streets. As a result, this section of the route was known locally by staff and enthusiasts alike as 'The Chinese Railway', although it would appear that the logic for this has to rank with other local expressions such as 'Going round Bill's mother's' when describing a circuitous journey!

Meanwhile, outbound trams continued south-westwards along Clevedon Road, at the back of Calthorpe Park, then swung round a left and right curve before entering Court Road, which was the last part of the common part of the two services.

Cannon Hill

On reaching Edward Road the 37 and 39 tram routes diverged at the Cannon Hill public house at a triangular track layout. The 37 to Cannon Hill crossed Edward Road and turned into the more affluent residential Cannon Hill Road. This was the start of a mile-long anti-clockwise loop via Edgbaston Road (where it passed the entrance to Cannon Hill Park), Willows Road (where the terminus was situated), and Hallam Street. From the latter, the 37 route went back to Edward Road, but this time at its junction with Lincoln Street. Going round similar large, one-way loops on other tram systems was sometimes known as 'Cannon Hilling', a term coined by Wingate H. Bett, the well-known ticket authority.

City-bound 37 route cars went straight across Edward Road into Lincoln Street, then at Balfour Street they were joined again by the inbound 39 Balsall Heath services coming from Moseley and Kings Heath.

Balsall Heath

At Court Road, the 39 route trams going to Moseley, Kings Heath and Alcester Lanes End parted from the 37 route and turned eastwards to the left into Edward Road and proceeded along a mixed Victorian residential and retail area. This was again single-line working, but trams regularly travelled in the opposite direction from Moseley Road, enabling them to get to either the Cannon Hill triangle from Moseley Road depot, or to undertake other depot workings to Lincoln Street, for the inbound Cannon Hill route. Depot workings used the tracks at the eastern,

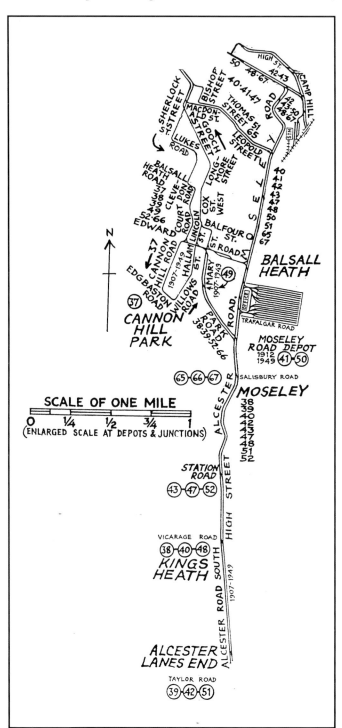

Moseley Road, end, which had been used for the circular Leopold Street-Balsall Heath service that lasted for only one week after its introduction on 1 January 1907.

The Balsall Heath trams travelled as far as Mary Street on their way out of the city before turning right and beginning the climb past the last of the Victorian terraces to the 49 route's short-working cross-over at Edgbaston Road. Beyond here the tram route continued into Park Road and passed through an area of better-quality houses and villas, built as a continuation of the expansion of Moseley when the railway was attracting the Victorian commuters.

The Balsall Heath tramcars emerged from Park Road into Alcester Road to join the trams that had started from High Street and had taken the more direct route along

Below Schematic diagram showing the routes of the 37, 39 and 41 tram services round 'the Chinese Railway', together with depot workings from Moseley Road depot. For clarity each outbound and inbound journey is shown as a separate line - the system map (*left*) shows which tracks were single and which double.

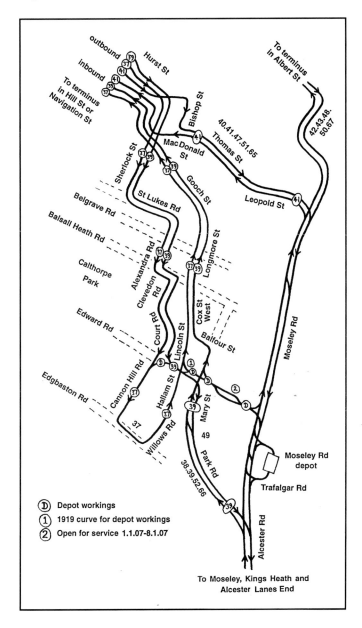

Moseley Road. Those going to Alcester Lanes End carried on along Alcester Road to nearby Moseley and Kings Heath.

On their return to the city, having descended Park Road and Mary Street, the inbound 39 route cars crossed Edward Road and turned left from Mary Street into a short length of Balfour Street. They then turned right into Lincoln Street where they joined the inbound Cannon Hill service and carried on through Cox Street West and into the start of the shopping area in Longmore Street.

The inner area of the city contained great swathes of sub-standard property and it was through an increasingly deteriorating landscape that the trams ran for some 42 years noisily, slowly, but unerringly. The houses in the Balfour Street and Cox Street West area were not the worst in the city, but not many years after the trams had finally been withdrawn this area was totally cleared, so that today the area to the north of Balsall Heath Road is virtually unidentifiable.

After crossing Belgrave Road, the trams returning to the city entered the busy Gooch Street, which after turning sharply to the north-west at Highgate Street, carried on for some 600 yards before regaining Sherlock Street. Here the trams turned right, crossing the outbound line of the Balsall Heath trams and almost immediately being joined, from MacDonald Street, by the city-bound trams returning from Leopold Street. At this point all the routes turned left into Hurst Street and climbed towards the city termini in Hill Street or Navigation Street.

High Street services

The High Street services were introduced on 6 September 1909 in an attempt to get passengers to the other side of the city centre. Inbound, the cars, which had climbed the Bull Ring's steep hill, passed the spiritual heart of Birmingham, the parish church of St Martin, before turning right alongside Oswald Bailey's Army & Navy stores and into Moor Street. Here the road again climbed, although this time not so steeply, as it left the bustling markets of the Bull Ring and passed the Great Western Railway's little Edwardian gem of Moor Street Station and, beyond that, the imposing Moor Street Warehouse. Once over the GWR railway bridge, the trams turned left into Carrs Lane, passing the mock-Tudor Corner public house on the left and the austere, classically inspired Congregational church of 1820.

The original terminus was in the short length of High Street between the top of Carrs Lane and the next turn to the right, which was Albert Street. This arrangement lasted until 1921 when a new central loading island in Dale End was used as the terminus, together with trams going to Coventry and Stratford Roads. Although the structure was impressive, its complicated tramcar access made it something of an operating millstone; thus in 1930 the Moseley Road trams were transferred to Albert Street outside the Beehive department store.

After leaving the distinctive canopied shelters at the top of Albert Street, the 'main-line' Moseley Road route to Alcester Lanes End, numbered 42, descended to the junction with Moor Street and turned right, passing some elegant early-Georgian houses, including, on the corner of New

Meeting Street, the former Dingley's Hotel, which had a particularly fine baroque frontage. At the bottom of Carrs Lane the outward-going trams completed their loop and met the inbound cars.

Having turned left into the Bull Ring, the Moseley Road trams followed the same route as the Coventry Road, Stratford Road and Warwick Road, and Stechford tram services; they descended past Digbeth Police Station at the corner of Meriden Street and proceeded along the busy shopping and warehouse area that was to be found in Digbeth. Digbeth was part of the Anglo-Saxon settlement of Birmingham and it was shortly before the original fording point of the River Rea that the Moseley-bound trams left the main thoroughfare and turned right into Rea Street, later to become better known as the home of the Midland Red's Digbeth bus garage and coach station.

A short length of the industrially lined Rea Street was traversed before the route turned left into the wide Bradford Street which led from the markets area towards Camp Hill. The tram route then climbed through an area of heavy industry before turning right into Moseley Road. This section, from Rea Street, followed the route of the 1884 steam trams.

Once into Moseley Road, the tram route passed Highgate Park and the splendid Elizabethan Stratford House before meeting the Leopold Street trams some 200 yards further on. Passing through Balsall Heath's late Victorian civic buildings, the straight run along Moseley Road led to the tram depot at Trafalgar Road, which had been opened for the Corporation takeover on 1 January 1907. Trafalgar Road was also the terminus of the usual Leopold Street services.

The nature of the route changed beyond the depot from an artisans' industrial area to the late-19th-century tree-lined residential suburb of Moseley. On the climb from the tram depot, the Balsall Heath route joined the main route at Park Road, and from here for the remaining two miles of the route to Alcester Lanes End, the 39 and 42 routes ran together. Moseley Village, at the junction with St Mary's Row, was reached next, with its high-quality shopping and air of prosperity. This was the turn-back point for the 65, 66 and 67 short-workings.

Beyond Moseley, the trams went uphill, passing Moseley Hall and Reddings Road, home of Moseley Rugby Football Club, before descending Welsh's Hill to the bridge over the Midland Railway line just east of Kings Heath station at Queensbridge Road.

The major shopping centre of Kings Heath was arrived at next; this had been a small village until the mid-19th century, but the extension of the CBT steam tram service on 1 February 1887 had the usual effect of encouraging urban growth. The former steam tram depot, coke yard and pits at Silver Street were passed on the right; this had been opened in 1887 and had a capacity of about 20 trams. After the closure of the steam tram system on New Year's Eve 1906 the depot was brought back into use by the Corporation on 1 April 1908; it continued to be used until 31 December 1911 when it was finally closed, although the building survives to this day. Further along the shop-lined High Street, past the steam tram terminus, was the Victorian All Saints church at the corner of Vicarage Road where, in later years, the Outer Circle, 11, bus route crossed Alcester Road South. It was also the turn-back point for the 38, 40 and 48 routes.

Beyond here the Alcester Road South section of the route began, descending gently to Howard Road before climbing the remaining half-mile to the terminus. This was just beyond Taylor Road at Alcester Lanes End, and opposite the Kings Arms public house, a hostelry always known locally as the 'Knob'. The terminus here was always busy, especially so when there was a meeting at Kings Heath dog track.

After the war the 42 route was usually worked by the open-balconied 401 Class, so there was frequently a mix of these and the 702 Class bogie cars working the 39 service to Balsall Heath at the terminus.

Balsall Heath: Navigation Street to Bromsgrove Street

Car 702, the first of the Brush-built bogie cars of 1926, stands in Navigation Street while waiting to leave on the 37 route to Cannon Hill. Just over the shoulder of the woman who is holding the child's hand can be seen the lower saloon door of the tram with the 'key' symbol of the Birmingham Municipal Bank etched on to the glass.

The Futurist Cinema is showing the film *White Woman* starring the English-born character actor Charles Laughton and Carole Lombard. She later married Clark Gable and was tragically killed in January 1942 when the aircraft in which she was travelling crashed in a blizzard in the USA. It is Monday 30 April 1934, the day that the British Government set up a study about the feasibility of a public television service; this in the fullness of time would eventually sound the death knell for the majority of Birmingham's cinemas. *J. Cull*

Right A positively gleaming car 415 stands at the Queens Hotel end of Navigation Street, working on the 41 route via Leopold Street; it will turn back outside the Moseley Road tram depot at Trafalgar Road. The car is ex-works, having been repainted on 5 April 1938; its condition suggests that the photograph was taken shortly afterwards. It is carrying an enamel advertisement for Whitbread's Ale and Stout, a common, conservative addition to numerous tramcars in the 1930s. This spring morning scene also has in the background a Guinness advertisement depicting the Spreading Chestnut Tree which was displayed in 1938.

Behind the tramcar can again be seen the roof of New Street Station which, when constructed, had been the largest canopy roof in the world with a span of 212 feet. It was badly damaged during an air raid on 26 October 1940 and was dismantled over a 15-month period to February 1947 by the aptly named Altitude Contracting Co Ltd of Birmingham. *R. T. Wilson*

In the late summer of 1949, car 328 stands against the kerb in Navigation Street next to the Finlay's tobacconist kiosk. Passengers continue to board this Moseley Road extra on the 70 route to Rednal while the driver and an inspector struggle with the points that will enable car 328 to use the crossover to gain John Bright Street. Meanwhile, car 435 unloads directly into Navigation Street after arriving from Moseley Road on the 41 route.

Towering over this scene once more is the Queens Hotel. This had been opened on 1 June 1854, but was rebuilt during 1911 and extended again in 1925 by building an extra two storeys on top of the original block. With the war came a slow loss of its importance. After suffering a general deterioration of the fabric of the station through lack of maintenance, by the time the last Moseley Road trams were running, the hotel's 'glory days' had gone. It was proposed to build a new hotel and offices in 1960 when the first rebuilding plans were announced for New Street, but these were altered and by 1964 the finalised plans were without the hotel and the old premises were finally closed in 1966. *F. N. Lloyd Jones*

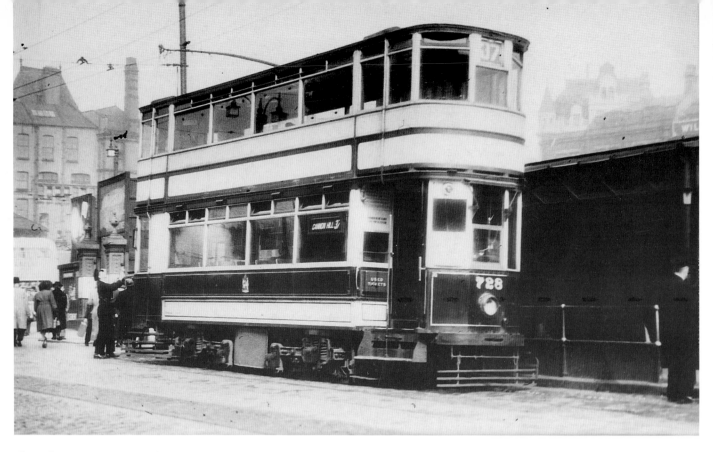

Above The 37 route originally terminated in Navigation Street, but after 1 May 1944 it started in Hill Street near the junction with Queens Drive, whose finial-topped gates are visible behind the tram.

Car 728 stands next to the shelters on 30 September 1947. This tram had returned to Moseley Road only one month before, having been at Witton depot since April 1939. The conductor is about to put the trolleypole on to the overhead while intending passengers to Balsall Heath and Cannon Hill board the tram. The side destination blind has been wound round the wrong way on the top spindle causing the lettering to slope backwards. *J. H. Price*

Below One can almost sense the wonderful smell of sulphur as a steam locomotive passes beneath the Hill Street bridge leaving behind a swathe of drifting smoke. Brand new Brush-bodied AEC Regent II 3106 (JHA 7), of Midland Red, is working into the city on the 130 route from Stourbridge in 1949. These AD2 types were the first to have the Midland Red-designed tin front, but their continued use on the main Hagley Road run from Birmingham came to a halt within a few years as, despite their modern looks, they only had an AEC 7.58-litre diesel engine, which left them very underpowered with a full load.

Car 717 is unloading passengers after working the 39 route in from Alcester Lanes End at Severn Street. The bomb-destroyed structures on the corner of Hill Street and John Bright Street are all that was left of the Malt Shovel public house, which received a direct hit on 19/20 November 1940. *F. N. Lloyd Jones*

Right The first of the UEC-bodied Spencer-Dawson oil and air brake cars unloads its passengers at the tram and trolleybus stop outside the Empire Palace in Hill Street at the junction with Smallbrook Street. It is on the 41 route and will follow the Leyland Titan PD2/1, 1701 (HOV 701), and the unusual Park Royal-bodied RT type, AEC 'Regent' III 1632 (GOE 632), up Hill Street to the terminus at Navigation Street.

The Empire Palace, the tall building with the round windows behind the tram, was opened in May 1894 and became part of the Moss Empire group of theatres. Unlike that graveyard of English comedians, the Glasgow Empire, the Birmingham theatre failed to survive the Second World War and was gutted in an air raid in 1941, leaving only the shell intact. The building was demolished in about 1951. *R. T. Wilson*

Below right If traffic conditions were like they are today, one can imagine an irate motorist's reaction at being stuck behind a tram that is unloading passengers in the middle of the road with the traffic lights on green! Fortunately it is February 1949 and the amount of traffic is minimal. However, the passengers who have just disembarked from car 729 and have walked out from behind the tram to cross Hurst Street would have had to have watched carefully as the large 1936 Austin saloon, probably an Eighteen, proceeds southward away from the city.

It can be seen that, like many of Birmingham's roads, Hurst Street was cobbled. What is interesting is the distinct change of pattern in the cobbles; as has already ben mentioned, the 18 inches or so on either side of the track was the responsibility of the Tramways Department, while from there to the kerb had to be maintained by the Highways Department.

The vaguely 'Arabian Nights' structure above the tram, apparently an added decorative feature to the products of the Brush Company, is in fact the top of the tower of the Birmingham Hippodrome; still extant today, it is the permanent home of the Birmingham Royal Ballet, a far cry from when the great Max Miller 'trod the boards' at the Hippodrome! *F. N. Lloyd Jones*

Left The Hippodrome tower is still visible as car 721 stands in Hurst Street at the junction with Bromsgrove Street on its way to Cannon Hill on 14 April 1938. The tracks leading in from the right used to carry the trams to Coventry and Stratford Roads, but it has been some 16 months since the most recent abandonment on Stratford Road, and the tracks are now only used for trams going to the works. This section of Hurst Street was wired for the inbound Coventry Road trolleybuses that would terminate in Station Street.

The Davenports public house is still trading today as the Australian Bar, but virtually every other building was swept away in the late 1980s to create the new Arcadian shopping precinct with its numerous Chinese supermarkets and restaurants. The entrance to the precinct is approximately where the following tram, car 428, working on the Leopold Street service, is standing. *H. B. Priestley*

Above At the bottom end of Hurst Street, away from the theatres around Smallbrook Street, was the start of the market and industrial area near the edge of the city. The large city public houses gave way to small Victorian corner 'locals', and the remnants of the worst of the mid-Victorian back-to-back houses that had escaped the bombs of the Second World War mixed, often somewhat uncomfortably, with piecemeal inter-war industrial development.

Car 442 has stopped at the bottom of Hurst Street and will take the line off to the left on the photograph, which will take it into Sherlock Street. The track to the right is the outward Leopold Street line. *F. N. Lloyd Jones*

Below Looking down Hurst Street towards the junction, we see where the 37 route to Cannon Hill and the 39 route through Balsall Heath and Park Road to Moseley and beyond parted company; the latter turned right into Sherlock Street, while the short section of Hurst Street between the cafe

and the public house in the centre of the picture took the 41 group of routes towards Leopold Street via Bishop Street and MacDonald Street.

The Blue Cafe on the corner of Sherlock Street is advertising 'a variety of sandwiches' - the three alternatives of meat, cheese and lettuce sound distinctly unappetising, but in 1949 there was still rationing, resulting in such meagre fare being offered.

Car 717 is about to take the right turn in front of the White Swan public house. This bogie tram, built in 1926 by Brush, was equipped with EMB bogies and GEC WT32H 40 hp motors; although a trifle slow compared to other bogie cars, these 702 Class trams were well suited to the Balsall Heath routes. This tram had been transferred from Witton at the end of August 1947 and it is seen towards the end of its 26-month sojourn at Moseley Road; after this depot closed 717 would go to Miller Street where it would work until the final day's operation of tramcars in Birmingham on Saturday 4 July 1953. *R. T. Wilson*

Leopold Street

Right A closer view of the far side of the junction in 1949, where the 41 route trams took the short length of cobbled road between the rundown, three-storeyed terraces, which were such a common feature of inner Birmingham, and the small workshops.

The White Swan public house seems more intent on advertising its allegiance to Ansells brewery than its name. This pub, standing on the southern corner of Hurst Street and Sherlock Street, dates from about the end of the 1920s and sits rather uncomfortably amongst the older run-down property.

Car 401, working on the 41 route, will pass the 1947 Bradford van and turn right into Bishop Street before turning left into MacDonald Street where it would meet the inbound cars. The latter would continue along MacDonald Street to meet Sherlock Street, to the right of the photograph, and turn right to join the route of the city-bound services via Gooch Street. *R. T. Wilson*

Right The only building to survive the demolition of the Victorian houses in the post-war period was the White Swan public house. It remains today surrounded by small factory units and open space and looks just as out of place as when it was the newest building in the area!

The importance of this section of Hurst Street is even less than in the days of the tram. It is now a one-way street with traffic coming from the Bishop Street direction. *D. R. Harvey*

Left On its outward-bound journey, car 416 has just turned from Bishop Street to meet the inbound track of the 41 route in MacDonald Street, and has stopped just beyond the Belisha beacon to set down and pick up passengers at the Barford Street stop. The Belisha crossing has no 'zebra' markings on the road, these being applied in 1951 and then generally only on roads with a tarmacked surface.

The extent of the damage done during the then recent wartime bombing in this area can be seen, with at least four sites being visible; a colloquial expression for these derelict areas was a 'bomb-building-site'. For children growing up in the early post-war years, these potentially dangerous places were secret dens, battlefields, football pitches and places in which to play hide and seek. Gradually, as the inner slum clearance schemes began, the old houses on either side of these sites were demolished and with them went the bombed sites.

Car 416 would proceed on its brief journey via the short length of Thomas Street towards its destination of Trafalgar Road. *R. T. Wilson*

Right Open-balconied car 430 has just descended Leopold Street on its way into the city on the 41 route in 1939, having just left the stop outside the school at the corner of Dymoke Street; the junction in the foreground is at Vaughton Street. The tram will turn slightly left and travel along Thomas Street and then into MacDonald Street.

Just visible above the hoardings is the St Martin's Estate. This experimental block of interconnected four-storey concrete-built flats was under construction from 1937 and was completed in 1939; 266 units were built and they marked a huge step forward in the thinking of Birmingham Council. In the inter-war period the Council had constructed a mere 355 new dwellings in the central wards of the city, when realistically a wholesale redevelopment of the housing in the inner city should have taken place during the 1930s.

The flats were not a success. Water seepage into the concrete blocks resulted in their previous prestigious fame quickly becoming replaced by notoriety. By the late 1970s the *Birmingham Evening Mail* referred to them as 'the rambling run-down warren of 266 problem flats'. In 1981 they were demolished! *D. R. Harvey Collection*

Left Car 426, working the 41 route, cautiously descends Leopold Street using its air and oil brake equipment to control, and where necessary, stop the tram on the 1 in 13 gradient. The fitting of this brake to the 401 Class in the latter half of 1913 raised the unladen weight of the trams by 12 cwt to 13 tons 2 cwt.

The Leopold Street trams ran through an industrial landscape as the route climbed the hill towards Moseley Road. In this inner area of Highgate there was a mixture of back-to-back houses dating from the middle of the last century as well as later Victorian terraces.

The true nature of the gradient can be assessed by the angle of the wartime Bedford OW lorry as it struggles up the hill. It is to be hoped that the parked American lorry will not obstruct the Bedford as the tram passes them both. *F. N. Lloyd Jones*

Below Four-wheeled tram 416 passes a parked 1938-registered Austin 10 on the steepest part of Leopold Street. On the right are the premises of Samuel Heath & Sons, whose brass foundry has been on this site since 1830. Throughout the inner part of Highgate, small specialised foundries and manufacturing companies grew up in the 19th century and around them developed the houses for their workers.

This scene was captured by Noel Lloyd Jones on the last day of operation of the Leopold Street service. The photographer, many of whose excellent pictures appear in this volume, comprehensively covered the Birmingham system on film from 1948 until 1953. Although now retired and living in Lancashire, he had a great affection for the Birmingham system, which is reflected in his photographs. *F. N. Lloyd Jones*

Top Car 419 is seen climbing Leopold Street on 10 June 1941, when working on the 37 route. Because of track damage this route was diverted via the 41 route on to Moseley Road and then via the depot working line in Edward Road to regain the Cannon Hill lines.

The tram's headlight is fitted with a blackout deflection mask as well as having its fenders painted white. The windows of the tram have been covered by anti-blast netting, which was glued on and made auxiliary conductors' travel even less enjoyable, as only a small square was kept clear. Things got so bad in the blackout that volunteers travelled on the trams and buses to call out to the passengers where they had got to. A temporary blast shelter has been made at the entrance to the industrial premises that the tram is passing. This and all the street furniture has been marked in white so as to stand out at night.

On this bleak wartime day in 1941, Hitler's deputy, Rudolf Hess, crash-landed his aeroplane near Glasgow and began one of the Second World War's most bizarre episodes. *W. A. Camwell*

Middle After leaving Moseley Road on the return journey into the city centre, car 426 has stopped on the brow of the steep section of Leopold Street. The compulsory red tram stop at the top of a descent was a regular safety feature on every route in the city, and here, with one of the steepest and longest climbs in Birmingham, over 600 yards, it was particularly necessary.

At the top of Leopold Street the land use changed and became far more residential. The houses were not the awful mid-19th-century back-to-backs, but the later 1880s style of terrace; these, however, still opened out directly on to the street.

The archway on the right was built to allow horse-drawn wagons to gain access to the workshops that lay behind the street facade. The area was typical of the central wards in the city, with nearly every corner having on it either a pub or a shop. *F. N. Lloyd Jones*

Bottom Once at the summit of Leopold Street the trams dropped gently to reach Moseley Road, where the four-wheel cars squealed as their rigid wheelbases took the tightly radiused turn. As at a number of sharp curves, water was used as a lubricant. The rail in Moseley Road had a small drain to allow the water to drain away.

Car 402, with three schoolboys riding on the balcony, is about to take the turn in front of the Perks iron and steel scrap merchants offices. This 1949 view shows the final state of the 401 Class cars that served the Moseley Road faithfully for all but a few months of their 37-year service life. At 29 ft 9 in long over fenders, these 1913-built trams were only 3 ft 9 in shorter than the first bogie cars delivered the following year. They originally had identical electrical equipment to the 512 Class, yet were 3¼ tons lighter, so their performance on Moseley Road was comparatively lively.

The 41 route would continue along Moseley Road only as far as Trafalgar Road. This route via Leopold Street was the shortest, and was the normal service after 1939 as the 40 route to Kings Heath only ran at peak periods, while the 51 route to Alcester Lanes End only had occasional journeys. Before the Second World War there was also a Sunday 51 service operated by 702 Class bogie cars. *R. T. Wilson*

Sherlock Street to Cannon Hill

Right A large Austin Eighteen taxi speeds past the Sherlock Street junction with Gooch Street (on the left) and overtakes car 729, which is on its way to Cannon Hill. Gooch Street was used for the inbound 37 and 39 routes, while the outward routes continued along Sherlock Street before turning left at St Lukes Road, which was the third junction after Gooch Street.

The run-down nature of this area can clearly be seen in this 1949 view. Areas of derelict land abound as testament to the bombing that took place in the area in 1940 and 1941, with huge wooden props being buttressed against walls in order to support the surviving sub-standard buildings for a few more years. Compared to the photograph of car 728 on page 79, it will be noticed that the buildings at the end of Gooch Street, in this 1949 view, have been demolished. *R. T. Wilson*

Above On the last day of operation, a rather run-down and worn-out-looking car 418 passes through the equally run-down and worn-out Balsall Heath area. It is turning from Sherlock Street into St Lukes Road on the outward 37 route, and the tight left-hand turn took the trams into a typical inner city area. The main roads tended to have premises that were both commercial and of a slightly better standard, often with ornate cornices, porched entrances and stone-faced brickwork such as can be seen on the building on the far corner of Sherlock Street and St Lukes Road. Once into the less prestigious roads, the quality of houses worsened. This, after 80 or more years of occupation, resulted in numerous areas in the city, including Balsall Heath, declining into squalor. Unfortunately the city council could not afford to demolish them all at once and throughout the early post-war period the Housing Department 'topped and tailed' houses that were basically unfit for human habitation in order to squeeze a few more years of use out of them.

The section of St Lukes Road west of Sherlock Street, to the left of the tram, was an important bus route, being used by the Inner Circle, 8 route, from 16 August 1926 until 27 September 1962, when the route was diverted to cross Bristol Road at Belgrave Road. *A. K. Terry*

Right The mid-19th-century houses on the north side of St Lukes Road still had remnants of Regency styling in their street elevations, which contrasted with the later residences on the southern side of the road.

Car 363 sets down two passengers in the gas-lit road just beyond the junction to the left with Varna Road. This part of Balsall Heath near to Pershore Road was known as the St Martins area, and was always regarded as being the 'better end' of this ward of Birmingham, being developed from about 1840 with 'exceedingly eligible villa residences'. The lands owned by the Moore family and that of the heirs of Rev Vincent Edwards in Balsall Heath were very quickly sold off for housing in increasingly small plots and increasingly spacious housing. This compares rather unfavourably with the controlled leasing of large plots in the nearby Calthorpe Estate.

The walls in front of the earlier houses to the right are later additions and

have capping stones made of the famous Staffordshire blue brick.

Today, with the exception of the distant school, all the buildings have gone, as has Varna Road itself. This was lost because of a reputation gained of being the unofficial night-life centre of Birmingham! Today, even the name has been erased to expunge from the residents' minds its former seedy notoriety. *F. N. Lloyd Jones*

Top A rather battered Brush-bodied bogie car, which entered service in December 1925 and is looking in need of a repaint and repair, prepares to move away after unloading its passengers in St Lukes Road at the junction of Belgrave Road during 1949.

The late-Victorian house to the left, whose decorative brickwork can also be seen on the right of the next photograph, belonged to a later period of housing development compared with the houses behind the disembarked tram passengers. The whole area had been ear-marked for redevelopment as early as 1942, although it would be nearly 20 years before the Highgate Comprehensive Development Scheme came to fruition.

Car 730 is working on the 37 route to Cannon Hill. This route, in common with most of the Moseley Road depot's services, was opened on Tuesday 1 January 1907 and remained virtually unchanged for all of its 42-year life. *F. N. Lloyd Jones*

Middle Working out of town in St Lukes Road, car 366 is being employed on the 39 route to Alcester Lanes End. Having just unloaded its passengers at Belgrave Road, the tram will travel straight across into Alexandra Road and travel about another 200 yards until reaching the next junction at Balsall Heath Road.

In this September 1949 view the Belgravia Hotel, within an area already in a state of run-down decline, was hardly a centre of opulence and was perhaps already being used by the first Commonwealth immigrants as their first lodgings.

As a tramcar due for withdrawal, 366 was transferred from Miller Street on 26 August 1949 to work out its last few weeks at Moseley Road depot, where it was broken up in October 1949. *R. T. Wilson*

Bottom An interchange of passengers takes place on the Cannon Hill-bound UEC-bodied, four-wheel car 418, which waits outside the Luxor Cinema in Balsall Heath Road in 1949.

Alongside the ornate exit of the cinema on the left is just visible an advertisement for the film *East Side of Heaven*, whose billing at the cinema seems to be impressing no one, not least the two short-trousered boys. The cinema opened in November 1913 as the Balsall Heath Picture House and changed its name to the Luxor in the 1940s. It closed in 1983.

Car 418 will turn hard right in front of the cafe into Clevedon Road. The cafe is actually on the corner of Jakeman Walk, which diverged at the same point, and this building occupies the whole block up to the next road, which is Cox Street West.

The tracks, as can be seen from the maps on page 60, were laid in adjacent streets with trams trundling up one narrow street, grinding around another tight turn and always going in only one direction, and it was this intertwining of the services in this part of Balsall Heath that led to them being given the nickname of 'The Chinese Railway' by tramway enthusiasts. The rear of another 401 Class open-balconied car can be seen at the next crossroads down, going into Longmore Street on its way into the city. *R. T. Wilson*

Left In this pre-war view, UEC-built car 547 has reached the southern end of Clevedon Road, and off to the left of picture is the entrance to Calthorpe Park. This was opened on Whit Monday 1857 by HRH The Duke of Cambridge in front of a crowd of 100,000 people.

The similar 512 Class bogie car in the distance is also following the left-hand curve of Clevedon Road while car 547, on leaving this stop, will take a bend to the right and enter Court Road. As can be seen, most of the area at this junction was made up of mid-19th-century terraces, but, as was typical of Balsall Heath and many other inner areas of Birmingham, these were interspersed with factories.

Car 547 entered service in 1913 and originally had open balconies. These were enclosed in July 1927 when the original Dick, Kerr KD19A 40 hp motors were replaced with the same company's DK30/1L 63 hp motors. The tram saw service until the penultimate day of tramcar operation in the city in a service life of 39 years. *L. W. Perkins*

Right Milk was delivered by horse and cart in Birmingham until well into the 1950s. One of the more extravagantly designed milk floats stands with its apparently patient horse between the shafts on the corner of Court Road and Edward Road. Opposite, outside Jones's electrical shop, the hoarding advertises that Nat Jackley, a comedian well-known for his rubber-necked eccentric walk, was appearing in *Piccadilly Hayride* at the Birmingham Hippodrome in October 1949, a theatre that car 365 would have passed on its way to Balsall Heath.

As can be seen, the intending suburban tram passenger had the difficulty of having to walk into the road in order to leave or, as in this case, board the tram. Fortunately, with only the milk float parked outside the public lavatories next door to the Cannon Hill public house and the Bradford van parked outside the electrical shop, there was, in this case, little danger.

Car 365 would turn past the milk float and into Edward Road before turning into Mary Street. *R. T. Wilson*

Right By 1993 the large stone-faced factory building to the left of the tram in the previous photograph has disappeared, as has the large four-storey factory in the photograph opposite of car 728; yet much of this end of Court Road at Edward Road remains untouched despite the passing of the trams and the growth of the trees in the intervening years. The cast-iron urinal next to the Cannon Hill public house has surprisingly survived despite not being exactly in its first flush of youth! Mr Jones's electrical shop is now King Creole's fast food shop, while the butcher's shop is now a Continental and Asian food store.

It was interesting that when I was taking this photograph a number of people in the street asked with incredulity what the point was in taking a photograph while standing in the middle of the road? None of them could believe that this somewhat quiet road was, at one time, part of a tram route. *D. R. Harvey*

BIRMINGHAM TRAMS 1933-53

Edward Road, the Cannon Hill loop and back to the city

Right Unlike the cars on the 39 route, those travelling on the 37 service to Cannon Hill branched right when they reached the end of Court Road, and, on crossing Edward Road, turned into Cannon Hill Road.

On 5 September 1949 car 728, in almost the same position as 365 pictured opposite and with its upper saloon windows open, turn right across the triangular junction.

In this view we see more of the row of shops on the corner of Edward Road and Court Road. One of them, Rawcliffe's, the newsagent and tobacconist, has three cigarette advertisements for 'Players Please' and one for Craven 'A'. In those far-off days, when nearly everyone smoked cigarettes, brand name advertising was not banned. *T. J. Edgington*

Left By contrast, car 419, working the 39 route, has just turned left from Court Road into Edward Road and is passing Jakeman Road on the right. The straight line in the foreground, forming the third side of this triangular junction, was used for depot workings.

The invalid carriage, fitted with a small motor-cycle engine and therefore licensed and carrying a number plate, is parked outside the Cannon Hill Studio, a photographers, whose portraits can be seen hanging in the window. The Edward Road area had a number of small shops and marked the boundary between the poorer-quality housing on the city side and the gradually improving quality towards Moseley. Therefore to have a photographer's studio in the area was not necessarily such a surprise; all these shops, like Hall's the ironmonger next door, with its galvanised dustbins and washing-tubs, would gradually disappear to be replaced by large supermarkets selling modern plastic equivalents.

The tram will continue on the single-line track away from the photographer to turn second right into Mary Street, and for the first time since leaving Sherlock Street become a two-way working again. *R. T. Wilson*

Left On Tuesday 10 June 1941 car 423 travels westwards along Edward Road towards Court Road at the Hallam Street junction, working the 37 route. Because of air raid damage the tram has been on a long detour via Leopold Street and Moseley Road before turning into Edward Road along the tracks used for access to and from Moseley Road depot. It will proceed to Court Road, then turn left on to its normal route in Cannon Hill Road just level with, and to the left of, the roof of the motor car proceeding towards the camera.

The tramcar is equipped with a complete set of wartime emergency features, including anti-blast mesh glued on to the windows. *W. A. Camwell*

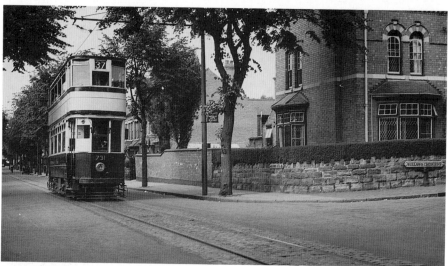

Above The single-line southbound working of the 37 route travelled for its last half-mile to the terminus round an anti-clockwise loop via Cannon Hill Road, having left the distant shops of Edward Road and entered the most residentially prestigious section of the route. This tree-lined area in Balsall Heath was developed at the very end of the 19th century; the bay-windowed terraced houses had small gardens, while decorative brickwork adorned their fronts. They echoed the developments in nearby Moseley as they were built to a grand scale with up to six bedrooms and with the large reception rooms downstairs having high ceilings with decorative architraves and ceiling roses.

Car 418 trundles past the unconcerned children playing with their bicycles as an audience of older children surveys the general scene from the vantage of the tram's balcony. *R. T. Wilson*

Above left The straight run down the 600 yards of Cannon Hill Road was only crossed once; that was at Willows Crescent, which, like the tram route, was similarly lined with the larger late-Victorian terraces. Unadorned Brush-built 40 hp tram 731 is at the last request stop in Cannon Hill Road. *W. A. Camwell*

Left Car 417 appears to have unloaded all its passengers at the compulsory stop at the junction of Cannon Hill Road and Edgbaston Road on a hot summer's day in 1931.

The vendor with the handcart is wearing a white coat and a satchel; his cart has the word 'Birmingham' just visible on it and it carries a large wicker basket. However, it is very difficult to see precisely what he is selling. Certainly the children seem unperturbed by his presence!

The 37 tram service finished its outward run by turning left into Edgbaston Road and passing the main entrance of Cannon Hill Park. Two hundred yards away to the left and beyond the River Rea is the Warwickshire County Cricket Ground of Edgbaston. *R. T. Wilson*

Right It is amazing how many times the fleet number of a tram is obscured on commercial postcards. A lamp standard, a cyclist and pedestrians are quite common, but the most regular offenders were the crew of the tram itself. They seem to delight in having a conversation when standing right in front of the car, usually at the terminus, but always in the middle of the road!

An unidentifiable member of the 1926 702 Class stands at the terminus in Willows Road, Balsall Heath, in about 1935. The purpose of the postcard is to show the new traffic island at the junction of Edgbaston Road and Russell Road (in the foreground); the Belisha beacons, first introduced in 1934, were put in place at about the same time so as to discourage pedestrians from crossing the junction via the roundabout.
Commercial postcard

Left Another view of the terminus in Willows Road. Standing at the Bundy clock, which, incidentally, had various positions at the terminus, is bogie car 725. It is late September 1949 and the Cannon Hill route has only a few days to run and would be replaced indirectly by the 48 bus service, although this did not use a one-way system in the same way as the trams. This left a number of streets on the so-called 'Chinese Railway' devoid of a bus service.
Lens of Sutton

Right Recently repainted Cotteridge bogie car 830 was used on Sunday 10 July 1949 together with a Miller Street four-wheeler, car 367, to operate an LRTL tour of the Birmingham system. It is seen here turning from Lincoln Street into Edward Road, using the curve which was put into position in 1919 for depot workings only. The tracks in the foreground are the inbound ones in Hallam Street from the 37 route terminus in Willows Road which car 830 had used before starting this manoeuvre.

Normal service trams working the 37 route continued along Lincoln Street, made famous for many years by the Ford car agency, Lincoln Street Motors, whose showrooms were situated there.

At the next junction, opposite the trees just visible in the far distance, was Balfour Street, where the inbound Alcester Lanes End cars on the 39 group of routes rejoined the Cannon Hill trams on their return journey into the city.
A. N. H. Glover

Left Returning to the 39 route, outbound bogie car 728 turns from Edward Road into Mary Street working towards Alcester Lanes End towards the end of its 26-month sojourn at Moseley Road depot, which began at the beginning of September 1947.

The tracks going straight over the junction just in front of the tram were used to get trams to and from Moseley Road depot on to the Balsall Heath routes; passengers were allowed on these depot workings, although not on official fare-paying journeys.

The Hillman in the background is the only post-war vehicle to be seen in this view. The gas lamps, as exemplified on the left, were to remain throughout the city until the mid-1960s, and the buildings that included George Le Resche's business of Balsall Heath Motors were swept away in the Balsall Heath redevelopments of the 1970s. *R. T. Wilson*

Below Looking run-down and shabby in the summer of 1949, inbound car 416 has descended Mary Street working on the 39 route and has stopped at the compulsory red stop before crossing Edward Road, seen in the foreground. The tram stands outside the Regency Dry Cleaners and barely gets a second glance from the three young women and the little boy in the pram.

The opposite side of Mary Street, behind the photographer, was one of the earlier developments in Balsall Heath with some small workshops and 11 houses being recorded in the 1841 census. Gradually the road and its associated buildings spread to the south up the hill towards Edgbaston Road and Park Road beyond. The nature of the housing changed, so that once the vicinity of the junction at Edward Road had been left, the buildings changed to a purely residential function of generally two storeys. *R. T. Wilson*

Bottom left The serried terraces of Victorian houses in Mary Street gave way to a strange group of houses just north of Edgbaston Road. This is on the sharp descent to the Strensham Road junction which bogie car 717 is approaching. The seven houses to the left were built with wrought-iron-balustraded balconies with delicate trelliswork that separated the walkways from each other. They look a little the worse for wear, but have been restored and are extant today. By way of contrast, the dismal row of three-storeyed houses and shops opposite that leads up to the junction with Edgbaston Road have all been demolished. Car 717, working the 39 route, is passing the cross-over where the 49 route trams turned back. *F. N. Lloyd Jones*

Below A City of Birmingham Tramways Company Kitson Steam Locomotive, number 73, built in 1894, is running firebox-first while towing one of the first series of Falcon bogie canopy-topped double-deck trailers. These were built in 1884 and were the only ones to have knifeboard seating in the open-sided upper saloon.

The trailer is displaying the route letter 'K' signifying that it is working on the Kings Heath via Balsall Heath route. The route was opened in July 1886 by the Birmingham Central Tramways Company; the steam trams operated from Hill Street and their route was largely followed by the replacement Corporation electric trams that took over on 1 January 1907. Alternate journeys normally turned back at the Edward Road-Mary Street junction and would display the destination letter 'B'.

On this sunny summer's day, probably around the turn of the century, the ensemble of loco and trailer stands in Park Road at the loop at Augusta Road. *M. Rooum*

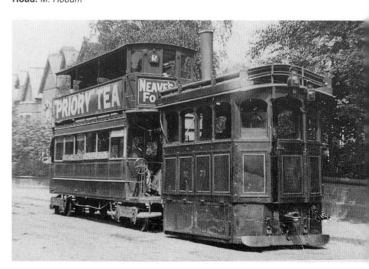

Right Car 448 has worked 'The Chinese Railway' on the 39 route through Balsall Heath and here emerges from Park Road into Alcester Road in 1949 (this junction is also shown in the photograph of car 418 climbing up from Moseley Road depot on page 91). The top of the climb up Mary Street can be seen behind the tram.

This junction was dominated by the large Victorian house that stood in its own grounds in the apex of Park Road and Alcester Road. It represented the largest type of late-19th-century development when Moseley vied with Edgbaston to be the most prestigious address around Birmingham.

Although the house has recently been demolished, much of this area remains the same today, its properties, which a few years ago looked decidedly worn out, being renovated and gentrified.

The tram will continue through Moseley Village and on to the Alcester Lanes End terminus some two miles away (see page 89ff). *R. T. Wilson*

Above A section of track that was used for service only during one week in January 1907, but was retained for another 49 years, was that in Edward Road which linked the section from Mary Street to Moseley Road. It was used solely for workings between the nearby Moseley Road depot and either the inbound or outbound 39 group of routes at Mary Street. At the next junction to the west, at Hallam Street, the inbound 37 route could be reached, while at the Cannon Hill public house at Court Road the outbound 37 service was accessible.

This link became important in the early years of the Second World War when bomb-damaged areas around the Balsall Heath area required the Cannon Hill service to operate outwards via Leopold Street and Moseley Road (see page 73).

Car 725 has just turned into Edward Road from Moseley Road in 1949. It is showing the 38 destination and will return from the city only as far as Kings Heath. *R. T. Wilson*

Right A Daimler COG5 bus speeds past along Moseley Road as the driver of 1925 Brush-built bogie car 719 uses his point-bar to alter the points at the end of Edward Road on Friday 26 August 1949 to enable the tram to right into Moseley Road and return to the depot. The tram has been recently repainted and is in sparkling condition, although the cast iron blue and orange enamel plate advertisement for Dewars whisky looks as if it has a fair amount of rust near the gutter drainage pipe; but then it may have been over 20 years old. The late 1940s equivalent of Mothercare is advertised on the tram: 'After the Stork - Little Toddlers' - but this appears to be a paper advertisement.

Car 719 would move to Miller Street on 10 September 1949, some three weeks before the abandonment, along with cars 716 and 721, and would be replaced by 301 Class four-wheelers 339, 365 and 366, which were exhibiting signs of ageing and were due for withdrawal. They ran out their time at Moseley Road, releasing the bogie cars that they replaced on a one-for-one basis. *T. J. Edgington*

Above left Car 438 is on its way into the city in Balfour Street, having just turned left from Mary Street in the distance; it is just about to take the right-hand curve into Lincoln Street where it will join the incoming cars on the 37 route via Cox Street West. It has already travelled 200 yards from Edward Road on the tortuous Balsall Heath inbound line and has over half a mile to go before rejoining the outbound tracks in Sherlock Street.

The close-knit communities that developed in areas like Balsall Heath almost made up for the social housing conditions. In areas such as this as many as 90 per cent of properties lacked indoor sanitation, and bathrooms were virtually unheard of; yet it was considered 'quite nice' to live in a two-up, two-down terrace house. The public baths, opened in Moseley Road in

1906 and built in the Flemish-Jacobean style favoured for many public utility buildings in Edwardian Birmingham, meant that often cleanliness was only a tram-ride away. *F. N. Lloyd Jones*

Above right Meanwhile, on inbound route 37, car 728 passes perhaps the last trees on its way in from the sylvan delights of nearby Cannon Hill. It is in Lincoln Street and at the distant three-storeyed corner shop will fork to the left into Cox Street West.

The sunny day cannot disguise the years of neglect and decay in this part of Balsall Heath. All would be swept away in the comprehensive redevelopment programme of the 1960s, which removed for ever roads like Cox Street West. The street had been named after a land-owning family in the area who could trace their ancestry back to 1608 when the area had been poor-quality farmland. Ironically, today much grassed open space covers large tracts of Balsall Heath, so the land use has gone almost full circle in nearly 400 years. *F. N. Lloyd Jones*

Left In the background of the photograph of car 418 outside the Luxor Cinema in Balsall Heath Road (page 71) can be seen an open-balconied tram going on its inward journey. Here, car 731 is about to perform the same manoeuvre crossing Balsall Heath Road from Cox Street West into Longmore Street beneath the stylishly embellished block of shops, the corner one having the large number 79 on it, visible above the tram. In the earlier photograph the same embellished frieze below the eaves can be seen.

The return route to the city altered noticeably from this point. The unending terraces of houses gave way to rows of small shops nearly all the way to the Sherlock Street junction almost half a mile away. *F. N. Lloyd Jones*

BIRMINGHAM TRAMS 1933-53

Above Having just crossed Belgrave Road from Longmore Street, Brush car 726 travels along the 50 or so yards from the junction in Gooch Street before taking the curve into the straight, 600-yard-long main section of the route that will take it to Sherlock Street. It is 1949 and the tram is in the last style of livery.

The reputation of the 'Brummie' with his flat accent, dry sense of humour and hard-working but unimaginative nature might be applied to the trams as well. Elsewhere, tram classes and designs were given interesting names. Liverpool had the 'Cabin Cars' and the 'Green Goddesses'; Glasgow had the 'Coronations' and the 'Cunarders'. All the Belfast trams built after 1920 were named after the general manager who was responsible for their construction, a tradition followed for a time in Leeds. In Birmingham odd trams were given names; for example, cars 451 and 452 were known as the 'Titanics' and 342 was the 'Armoured Car'. Then there were the 'Peckhams' and the 'Brill-Maleys' and of course the 'Lightweights', cars 842 and 843, but they were hardly names to conjure with! Yet here is car 726, one of a fairly substantial order of 30 built by Brush in 1925, known within the Tramways Department as '32Hs'! *F. N. Lloyd Jones*

Below Having turned the sharp left-hand bend in Gooch Street, the trams went though a shopping area that consisted of small family concerns or local chains of shops such as the Wrensons grocery chain.

Car 716 passes on the left a Birmingham-registered Austin Seven of 1937 vintage that is parked facing the wrong direction, while parked on the other wide of Gooch Street is a Morris Eight. The tram has worked in from Cannon Hill and is at the junction with Hope Street.

The Gooch Street route had originally been constructed by the Birmingham Central Tramways Company as a steam tram service; this had been opened on 19 July 1886 through Balsall Heath and joined up with the Moseley Road service. *F. N. Lloyd Jones*

Left At the city end of Gooch Street, at the junction with Sherlock Street, inbound trams from Balsall Heath and Cannon Hill turned right and crossed the 'out of city' lines.

The air of dereliction, even compared with the view of 729 earlier in 1949 as it travelled along Sherlock Street (see page 70), is even more noticeable. The corner buildings have been demolished and several others lie empty awaiting their fate. Bogie car 728 is about to leave the compulsory stop in Gooch Street and is passing the police telephone kiosk on the corner. The only building from this era left here today is the public house on the corner of Gooch Street and Barford Street. *R. T. Wilson*

Moor Street to Moseley Road

Right Open-balconied, four-wheel car 441, built in 1912 by UEC, passes the mock-Tudor-fronted Atkinson's public house, The Corner, as it turns from Moor Street into Carrs Lane in the summer of 1949. It has turned just ahead of an inbound Coventry Road trolleybus belonging to the 17-66 Class of Leyland TTBD2 six-wheelers, and will inch its way past a 1949 Daimler CVG6 on the 37 route to Hall Green and 1948 Daimler CVD6 1790 (HOV 790), which is picking up passengers for the 44 service. Beyond that bus in another Leyland six-wheel trolleybus working the 94 route. Unlike the Daimler COG5 seen at the far end of Carrs Lane, tram 441 will twice turn right; firstly into High Street and then into Albert Street outside the Beehive store.

Car 441, a 40 hp-motored tram, is mounted on 7 ft 6 in Mountain & Gibson trucks and belongs to the 50-strong 401 Class. These looked very similar to the preceding 361 Class, although they were considerably heavier as they were fitted with the air and oil brake. *R. T. Wilson*

Left Another tram, car 403, turns into Carrs Lane at The Corner public house before making its way up towards High Street, working the 42 route, also in 1949. The tram will have dropped most of its passengers off at the Bull Ring end of Moor Street as, at this time, the markets area was far more accessible then it is today. The present-day road system left the Bull Ring Centre and the associated markets very isolated from access by public transport. This has always been the Achilles' heel of the 1960s redevelopment of the traditional market centre of Birmingham and, in recent years, the resulting redevelopment has always been under the uncertainty of possible wholesale rebuilding.

This photograph of car 403 shows the traditional nature of these trams. They were the last four-wheel cars to be purchased new by Birmingham Corporation Tramways Department in 1912. Yet, when built they were at the forefront of tram-car development; the subsequent 512 Class of bogie cars, also constructed by UEC, which were built the following year, were only 4-foot-longer versions of the same basic open-balconied design. *F. N. Lloyd Jones*

Right Carrs Lane was an important focus of public transport in Birmingham's city centre, being used by routes coming in from the south and south-eastern sides of the city. The trams and trolleybuses would turn right into High Street and then right again to their termini in Albert Street before leaving the city centre via another right turn back into Moor Street.

Empty car 444, on the short-working 50 route from Trafalgar Road, leads Leyland TTBD2 six-wheel trolleybus 48 (OC 1148) past the imposing Town Mills warehouse as they climb Carrs Lane towards High Street. Behind the second trolley-bus is a similar procession, with car 441 and trolleybus 35 (OC 1135) leading a Daimler COG5 that is negotiating the Moor Street turn outside The Corner public house (as seen above). The derelict site on the right, used for parking cars, was created on the night of 9-10 April 1941 when a force of 250 bombers dropped 650 high explosive bombs and 170 sets of incendiaries on the city. This destroyed a lot of buildings in the High Street and New Street area, including these in Carrs Lane, and killed or injured some 1,121 people throughout the city. *R. T. Wilson*

BIRMINGHAM TRAMS 1933-53

Above On a miserable Sunday, 17 July 1949, car 402 approaches the top of Carrs Lane when working on the 42 route. It is passing the interwar-built shop of Brodericks, a bedding and furniture store, before turning right into High Street. One of the few early-19th-century buildings in this part of the city to escape the bombing raids of 1940 and 1941 still stood opposite Carrs Lane in the form of Hilton's clothes store. By way of contrast, car 402 has on its balcony dash an advertisement for E. R. Green, a ladies' coat and dress shop in Kings Heath which would outlast Broderick's, Hilton's and the tramcar by at least 30 years. *C. C. Thornburn*

Below UEC four-wheeled, open-balcony car 363 was allocated to Moseley Road depot from October 1948 until September 1949. The depot's normal allocation of four-wheelers was the similar-looking 401 Class, but from early in the Second World War there were always between four and six of the ubiquitous 301 Class allocated to the depot.

The tram is seen crossing into Dale End before turning back into Martineau Street on a Villa Park special in the winter of the 1948-49 season; it is passing in front of the subterranean gentleman's lavatory at the bottom of Bull Street. It is attended by two members of the BCT Inspectorate, one in the foreground in front of the Washwood Heath bogie tram standing in Dale End and the other seemingly 'walking' 363 over the cross-over. The policeman on point duty seems to have the attention of the pedestrians, but standing as he is at the bottom of Martineau Street, next to the temporary buildings on the bomb-site, he appears to be away from the manoeuvres of the trams.

Behind car 363 in High Street is a Coventry Road six-wheel trolleybus and a Daimler CVD6 of 1948 vintage working the recently introduced 54 route from Stechford. *F. N. Lloyd Jones*

Right This fine study of car 389 as it turns from High Street into Albert Street, in front of the RAF recruitment office on the first floor and the Corner House confectionery shop, shows the car still to be in the pre-war lined-out livery. The delicate wrought ironwork on the open balcony seems at odds with the rest of the functional design. The open balcony was necessary because of the Board of Trade's refusal to allow the operation of narrow-gauge, totally enclosed, four-wheel double-deck tramcars. These 301 Class cars were among the first in the country, when built in 1912, to be fitted with Dick, Kerr DK13A 40 hp motors and Preston 'flexible axle' swing-yoke 7 ft 6 in wheelbase trucks. They were also lower than any preceding Birmingham trams, being only 15 ft 7½ in high, which enabled them to pass beneath the low bridges at Aston Station and Selly Oak.

Car 389 continued in service until the closure of the Moseley Road trams on 1 October 1949 and was broken up at Moseley Road depot in December of that year. *F. N. Lloyd Jones*

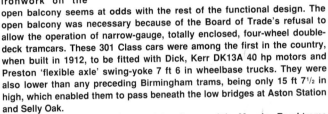

Top The main city centre to Alcester Lanes End service was numbered 42, but it had numerous short-workings. Here car 448 stands at the impressive shelters in Albert Street outside the Beehive store. The Beehive was an independent department store advertising itself as 'A Warehouse for the People'. It sold everything from household goods to baby clothes, and for many years retained its wonderful overhead money and bill-paying cable system whereby small brass canisters were sent to a central point in the store for all bills and change to be dealt with. The Beehive, after many years of contraction and struggle, closed on Leap Year Day 1972, having been in business for just over a century.

Car 448 is seen on Saturday 10 September 1949 in company with Daimler COG5 bus 1057 (CVP 157), which was built in 1937 and would be one of 41 such pre-war buses that would survive until 1960. It is working on the 54 route to Stechford, which itself had only been introduced just 11 months earlier when the 84 tram service had been abandoned. *F. N. Lloyd Jones*

Middle After leaving the Albert Street terminus, the Moseley Road trams turned back into Moor Street. Just before the former Great Western Railway station of that name, the traffic in Moor Street had to negotiate the rise in the ground as the road passed over the 596-yard railway tunnel that gave the railway access from the south to Snow Hill Station on the other side of the city centre.

Here car 403 crests the rise when working towards the Bull Ring, in Moor Street on the 42 route in the early part of 1949. *F. N. Lloyd Jones*

Bottom On its way to Kyotts Lake Road on Saturday 4 July 1953 is Brush totally enclosed GEC WT32H 40 hp bogie car 728. This tram had been one of Moseley Road depot's allocation until 1 October 1949 when it was transferred to Miller Street. It is seen here making its last journey to the works for scrapping, and was one of 23 cars to be broken up in the early part of August 1953.

Towering above the surrounding buildings is Moor Street Warehouse, which was owned by the family concern of A. J. Norton. After 50 years of trading it closed in March 1964 and the building was destroyed in a fire on 14 August 1965. This was the worst fire in the city since the Halfords blaze ten years earlier, and needed 100 firemen and 23 appliances to control the conflagration.

The tram is passing Moor Street Station, which was opened by the Great Western Railway on 1 July 1909 and helped to relieve Snow Hill from the increasing burden caused by commuter traffic using the lines from Leamington Spa and Stratford-upon-Avon. The railway station had a pleasant if unassuming entrance that lacked the grandeur and romance of Snow Hill and the sheer size of New Street and always looked an uncomfortable adjunct to the transport system of Birmingham. It would have been much more at home in a smaller town where its glazed bricks and little kiosks were an Edwardian delight. The station was replaced on Monday 28 September 1987 and at present it is mothballed with a view to preserving its Edwardian glory. *T. J. Edgington*

BIRMINGHAM TRAMS 1933-53

Right On the same wet Sunday as seen on the previous page, 17 July 1949, four-wheel car 420 speeds up Moor Street going eastwards over the Moor Street tunnel. In the distance is the Woolworth building on the other side of the Bull Ring in Spiceal Street. The 42 route, on which car 420 is working, will then turn left into Carrs Lane in order to reach its terminus in Albert Street.

This air and oil brake car retained its pre-war livery until withdrawal on the last day of operation on 1 October 1949. After a 37-year service life at Moseley Road depot it would be broken up there in December of that year by George Cohen & Son Ltd.

Moor Street was one of Birmingham's oldest streets and the name is a corruption of 'moledum', meaning a mill. In fact, a mill existed in the area up to the end of the 17th century and after that the road became important as a routeway below the hill on which the centre of Birmingham stood, linking the southern routes into the city with those leading out to Aston and the Tame valley. The mid-19th-century shops behind the tram survived until the late 1950s when the Inner Ring

Road Scheme, inspired by Herbert Manzoni, swept them away leaving only a small section of the original route fronting Moor Street railway station extant. *C. C. Thornburn*

Below The Bull Ring, until it was emasculated by the redevelopment of the 1960s, was the spiritual and historical centre of Birmingham. It was the traditional market place of the city and could trace its origins back to the Domesday Book, when the original settlement of Birmingham on this site was worth 20 shillings. The Bull Ring was the area between Moor Street, on the extreme left of this 1949 view, and Park Street, approximately where the M&B public house on the skyline is situated. To the right is the parish church of St Martin, which was one of Birmingham's main medieval buildings, being first mentioned in 1263, but was rebuilt between 1873 and 1875 by the versatile local architect, J. A. Chatwin. He earned a reputation for

being 'thorough but uninspired' as far as his Gothic rebuilding of churches was concerned. St Martin's, with its imposing tower, stands today as an ecclesiastical and architectural focus over the markets area of the city.

Car 414, one of four of the 401 Class to have extended UEC trucks of 8 ft 6 in wheelbase, turns out of Moor Street on the 42 route and passes the Midland Red BMMO FEDD parked in front of St Martin's. The rather uninformative destination blind on the 1949 bus, 1865 (HOV 865), shows that this Daimler CVG6 is on its way to the Hall Green terminus, working over the route of the former 17 tram route that had been abandoned some 12 years previously. The tram is about to descend the Bull Ring on its way to Digbeth and the turn into Rea Street, and is being met by similar UEC four-wheel car 443 which precedes Leyland six-wheeled trolleybus 24 (OC 1124) working into Albert Street from Coventry Road on the 94 route. It will be seen that the tram is using the common positive wire of the trolleybus overhead. *R. T. Wilson*

Left On a bright summer's day in 1949, car 415, painted in the 1946-style livery, descends the Bull Ring on the 42 route. It has turned out of Moor Street, on the corner of which stands the impressive early-19th-century building occupied by the Oswald Bailey Army & Navy Stores, and behind it is the upper part of the Bull Ring. In this bustling heart of Birmingham was a whole range of shops that carried on down the hill into Spiceal Street.

Standing opposite the Midland Red utility bus in the distance, and dwarfing these shops, was the huge Market Hall built in 1833 to the design of Charles Edge. This received a direct hit in an air raid by incendiaries on 25 August 1940, but for the next 23 years the roofless shell continued to serve as a market. For many years two disarmed German bombs stood on plinths and served as collection points for various charitable events until the building was demolished in January 1964.

The whole of this area was in dire need of redevelopment after further ravages of war and in the early 1960s was completely swept away by the Bull Ring Centre and the Inner Ring Road. *F. N. Lloyd Jones*

Below right Digbeth in about 1935 was a narrow bustling thoroughfare into which funnelled all the tram routes going towards the Bull Ring. These were the Stratford and Warwick Road routes, the Coventry Road and Stechford services and those Moseley Road routes that started from Albert Street.

Car 433 is working on the 50 route short-working to Moseley Road and the depot, and is just passing Digbeth Civic Hall on the right. It will shortly turn to the right and follow the Midland Red single-decker into Rea Street.

The tram is being followed by what appears to be a Brush-bodied AEC Regent 661 of 1929. In the distance, at the rear of a queue of trams waiting to cross the Moat Row-Meriden Street junction, is Leyland TTBD2 six-wheeled trolleybus 35, OC 1135, working on the 92 route to Albert Street.

The tall, grime-encrusted buildings on the left separated Digbeth from Midland Red's Digbeth garage, and when these properties were cleared the site was used as a hard standing for that company's buses for a number of years until the mid-1950s. *D. R. Harvey collection*

Below Car 441 stands in Digbeth outside the Old Bulls Head M&B public house. Like 433 above, it is about to turn right into Rea Street, this time on the 42 route to Alcester Lanes End. The following Leyland TTBD2 MCCW-bodied trolleybus on the 92 route still has a cream roof. Roofs were painted a muddy brown on all buses during the Second World War, and a modified light shade of khaki was retained after the end of hostilities as it was harder-wearing than the original all-over cream. Therefore this is a pre-war view, showing that the UEC-bodied four-wheeler, even after over 20 years of service, was in remarkably good condition.

The Old Bulls Head survived the road-widening and redevelopment of the 1950s in Digbeth and is still used as a hostelry today. On the traction pole on the right is the Selector Relay Switch box, which connected the actuating mechanism between the overhead-line switch and the points on the track for trams going into Rea Street. Also on the traction pole is one of the hexagonal trolleybus stops, just above the oblong tram stop. *W. J. Haynes*

Top The Digbeth end of Rea Street was very run down after years of neglect. A pre-war road-widening scheme was frozen for nearly 20 years and this contributed to the planning blight in the area. Interestingly, however, the buildings that were cleared to enable Digbeth/Deritend to become a dual carriageway did not include the garage advertising over-hauls seen just behind the tram. This site is still awaiting development, although during the summer months it is occasionally used as an overspill car park for coaches using the Digbeth coach station.

Car 431, approaching the city on the 42 route, led something of an unusual early career. It ran as a single-decker, initially as 'The Committee Car' for the Birmingham Tramways Committee and subsequently as a single-deck tractor pulling ex-CBT car 509 on the Nechells route. After this continental-inspired trailer operation ended, car 431 was fitted with a BCT-built top-cover at Kyotts Lake Road Works in May 1923. This upper saloon was not built with top-light windows, which made the car easy to identify as the only member of the class so fitted. It had the dubious distinction of operating the last car on the 41 route via Leopold Street on the final night, Saturday 1 October 1949. *D. R. Harvey collection*

Middle Rea Street, where the trams passed the Midland Red bus garage, was the link between the tracks in Digbeth and those in Bradford Street. The garage had opened on 3 July 1929 and gradually became the largest of Midland Red's garages, having an allocation of over 120 buses.

The Digbeth area of Birmingham was the original crossing point of the River Rea, which flows behind the mainly Victorian shops and factories fronting the south-eastern side of Rea Street. Although obviously having seen better days, the character of Rea Street, small factory units mixed with warehouses and specialised retail outlets, did produce a rich and lively feel to this heart of industrial Birmingham.

UEC oil and air brake car 444 is working on the 42 route to Alcester Lanes End on 19 March 1949. The tram has its own separate overhead from the Coventry Road to Station Street trolleybuses, and this complicated overhead wiring was to last after the closure on 1 October 1949 of the Moseley Road tram routes to serve the 93 trolleybus service that ran until the last day of June 1951. The tram lines remained wired up until the final closure so as to enable tramcars to be transferred to and from Kyotts Lake Road Works off Stratford Road. *A. Yates*

Bottom Car 406 turns from Bradford Street into Rea Street in front of the Anchor Inn public house on 24 July 1949. It is painted in the post-war livery, in which nearly all of this class were repainted. Although with only just over two months service left in front of it, it looks in good condition.

In the background, at the far end of Bradford Street, is the impressive Smithfield market on the corner of Moat Row and Moat Lane. This was designed by the then Borough Surveyor, W. Spooner Till, in 1883. It had round-arched lower-floor windows and well-designed wrought iron main gates set in red brick walls. This huge Victorian building stood on the site of the medieval manor house belonging to the de Bermingeham family and was eventually demolished. *G. F. Douglas*

Left Once the Moseley Road cars had turned left from Rea Street into Bradford Street they were faced with a half-mile straight run out of the Rea valley. Bradford Street, built in the 1770s, was named after a landlord of the time, one Henry Bradford, a timber merchant and prominent Quaker, who lived in Old Square, and linked the turnpikes coming into Birmingham from the south with the market area around Moat Row, just below the Bull Ring. It had once been a drovers' route into the then enlarging town, accounting for its straightness and width.

The 19th-century growth in industrial development in the Digbeth and Deritend area somewhat altered the urban structure of the area and it became one of the major industrial areas of Birmingham. Yet, despite the area's dramatic change from an agrarian lifestyle to heavy industry, the road itself retained its original wide character.

Car 442, working on the 42 route, has just descended Bradford Street and is about to turn right into Rea Street. This particular car was one of only 23 of the 401-450 Class to be fitted with the quieter helical gears. *A. Yates*

Left At the top of the steep climb up Bradford Street, the Moseley Road trams turned right into Moseley Road. Turning out of Moseley Road with a full load, in front of the Shepherds Rest public house, is car 407, one of the usual UEC-bodied, Mountain & Gibson four-wheel truck cars, fitted with the Spencer-Dawson air and oil brake and one of only three cars in the class to receive the final plain-style numerals at both ends.

The Shepherds Rest was a most aptly named hostelry, with Bradford Street's origin as a drovers' route. Certainly, as late as the 1870s animals that had been driven to market were penned up in Bradford Street before being consigned to the abattoir. At the bottom of Bradford Street, adjacent to the markets, was the Drovers' Arms. *R. T. Wilson*

Left On 20 August 1949 car 729, one of the GEC 40 hp '32H' Class of bogie cars, built by Brush, turns into Moseley Road on the 42 route. The tram had been assembled in 1925 at Moseley Road depot, and within two years, in common with the rest of the 702-731 Class, it was allocated to that depot. With the wholesale redistribution of cars that occurred after the Hockley abandonment on 2 April 1939, the entire class went either to Miller Street or Witton depot.

On the night of 4 December 1940 nine of the class were so severely damaged that they never ran again after the roof of Witton depot collapsed on them. Ironically all these nine damaged cars were stored for the duration of the Second World War at Moseley Road. One further tram, 771, was destroyed in April 1941 during the air road on Miller Road on 31 August 1947, after a further re-sorting of the tram fleet caused by the Ladywood abandonment. Tram 729 survived until the final Erdington closure of 4 July 1953, and is seen here, freshly painted, among the mixed Victorian industrial and residential frontages that characterised the Moseley Road area. *T. J. Edgington*

Below left The true run-down squalor of the three-storeyed back-to-back terraces in inner Birmingham can be seen here in Moseley Road. The tunnel entries alternating with the front doors usually led to a courtyard behind with communal lavatories, water pumps and wash-houses. The back-to-backs that faced the street gave a false indication of artisan prosperity, with their embellishments of entablatures and architraves. This was a reminder of the days when Victorian entrepreneurial landowners squeezed as many properties as possible on to their land in order to make as much profit from the investments as they could. Construction of back-to-back housing became illegal under the 1870 Housing Act, and in Birmingham at least, unlike Leeds for example, such appallingly mean housing was succeeded by the later, better quality tunnel-back terraces.

Car 412, working the 48 route in 1949, makes its way past these dismal rows of houses that survived until the 1950s just short of the junction with Bradford Street. Travelling along Bradford Street in the distance is a Daimler COG5 with a BRCW body going into the city on one of the Stratford Road services. *F. N. Lloyd Jones*

BIRMINGHAM TRAMS 1933-53

Right The post-war dereliction, due to bombing raids during the Second World War, left Moseley Road with a number of abandoned areas of waste ground. Car 438 is seen meeting identical car 424 at the Moseley Street junction in 1949. Car 438 has just passed the entrance of Highgate Park to the left of the picture. This opened on 2 June 1876 and had the unfortunate distinction of receiving over 200 bombs during the Second World War. Opposite the park and to the right of the photograph were built some gracious and impressive houses for Birmingham's manufacturers who saw the Highgate area as a haven from the nearby smoky, industrial areas that gave them their wealth. *R. T. Wilson*

Below right The only remnants left in Moseley Road from the previous photograph are the kerbstones that form the entrance to Highgate Park in the left foreground. In the distance can also be seen the high tower of one of the factories just off Bradford Street, but everything else has disappeared. Alexander-bodied Scania N113DR 3235 (H325 LOM), belonging to West Midlands Travel, is working the 50 route, which followed the 42 route service to the King's Arms at Alcester Lanes End and then to the Maypole. This was for many years the terminus of the tram-replacement bus services, but once the Druids Heath municipal housing estate was developed in the mid-1960s, the service was extended to this former area of green belt land.

Moseley Road still retains its mixture of industrial and residential land use, but the 19th-century buildings, with the exception of the odd public house, have largely disappeared and have been replaced by modern brick-built low-rise offices and flats. *D. R. Harvey*

Below Just visible in Stratford Place is the early-17th-century timber-framed and plaster-walled Stratford House. Built in 1601 for Ambrose Rotton and his wife Bridget, it is a typical Warwickshire farmhouse of the period of a sort that would have been built by a prosperous yeoman.

That Stratford House survived the subsequent agricultural land enclosures and the gradual early-19th-century urban growth of the Balsall Heath area is extremely surprising. The land immediately behind the house was used for the Birmingham & Gloucester Railway's passenger terminus from 17 December 1840, and later became the Midland Railway's goods yard. A single tramline off Stratford Place ran into Camp Hill goods station as it was from here that permanent way material such as ballast, granite paving-blocks and cement were transported to the BCT tramway system. A notable event in terms of the yard's tramway links was that the 702-731 Class were delivered between September 1925 and January 1926 to Camp Hill from Loughborough by the Brush Company. The upper and lower saloons were transported separately and the two halves were hauled along Moseley Road by horse-drawn low-loaders to Moseley Road for assembly.

Car 417 trundles between the large advertising hoarding and the Austin K2 furniture removal van on a winter's day in 1948 on its way out of the city. *D. Sanders collection*

Left Once the trams had left Stratford Place on the 42, 48 and 50 routes that had come via Bradford Street, they met the 40 and 41 routes that arrived at Moseley Road from Hill Street terminus via the steep hill in Leopold Street. Car 416, one of the Moseley Road depot's UEC-bodied, 54-seat, 40 hp four-wheelers mounted on Mountain & Gibson 7 ft 6 in trucks, passes the junction of Moseley Road and Leopold Street on 17 September 1949, just a fortnight before all the Moseley Road group of routes were abandoned. It is carrying a fairly full load despite its down-at-heel state. The far-end dash panel has a large dent in it and the paintwork shows, by its condition, that it is some four years since the tram's last repaint. Thirty-four of the 50 cars of the 401 Class were repainted between September 1946 and February 1949, leaving the remainder, including 416, to soldier on in an increasingly deteriorating state. *T. J. Edgington*

Middle The cobbled road surfaces of our major cities are today just a memory, but for normal vehicular traffic at the time of this photograph, September 1949, it was a major source of wear and tear. The suspension of cars and lorries was constantly flexed as the surface was not flat but often rose and fell in a series of sickening lurches. When wet the setts became an ideal surface on which to practise the art of skid control. Finally, there was the incessant drumming through the tyres.

The early post-war Austin 10 waits behind tram 366, which is painted in the pre-war livery. Ahead, car 329, the only tram at that time in Moseley Road's allocation not to carry advertisements, stands just before the junction with Leopold Street. Car 434, approaching the junction from the other direction on the 41 route, was one of the few members of the 1912-built 401 Class to be modified, being temporarily fitted with a Brush truck in May 1920 and subsequently an extended version of the standard Mountain & Gibson truck with an 8 ft 6 in wheelbase.

In this view it can also be seen that, although we are only about a quarter of a mile from the appalling properties near Bradford Street, the quality of the housing built in the third quarter of the 19th century improved enormously with the out of city growth of two-up, two-down terraces. *R. T. Wilson*

Bottom Working the city-bound 42 route, car 387 fills up with passengers in Moseley Road just north of the Highgate Road/Belgrave Road junction. The distant advertisement is for Swallow raincoats, and it was at that point, at Montpelier Street, that the entrance to the down side of Camp Hill passenger station was situated.

The pre-war Morris 10 cwt van parked just beyond the road junction appears to be delivering to the newsagent and tobacconists shop next to the Lloyds Bank, which was on the Highgate Road corner. The newsagent seems to be attracting more window shoppers than customers on this cold, sunny afternoon in early 1949.

The tram was one of only a very few to escape the mass breaking up of Moseley Road's allocation when its routes were abandoned. Car 387 was transferred to Witton depot on 16 September 1949 and would survive for another year. *F. N. Lloyd Jones*

BIRMINGHAM TRAMS 1933-53

Top Moseley Road rarely allowed for any really fast running until beyond Kings Heath, but the section between Belgrave Road and Edward Road did allow for a burst of speed. The open-balconied 401 Class were equipped with only 40 hp Dick, Kerr DK13A motors, but a spirited ride could be taken on sections of street track such as this. Car 442 had been fitted with Hoffman axle roller bearings in December 1945, which gave the car a smoother, quieter and slightly faster ride. The tram is just about to pass a 1939 Huddersfield-registered Ford Prefect that is parked on the corner of Lime Grove just opposite the Balsall Heath baths and library. Just visible above the tram through the trees is the decorated west tower of St Paul's church. This Gothic-styled church was consecrated in 1853 and pulled down in the 1980s, a decade that also saw the construction of Haden Way, part of the Middle Ring Road Scheme. This diverted the line of the main road into the city away from Moseley Road behind the buildings to the left of this view.

In the far distance, coming from the Belgrave Road traffic lights, is a 1949 Leyland Titan PD2/1 with a Brush body. This bus is working on the 35 route, which ran an express limited stop service to the Maypole over the tram route. *F. N. Lloyd Jones*

Middle Cars 431 and 435 pass Horrell & Bowman's Triplex depot at No 514 Moseley Road in July 1949. These two open-balcony cars show clearly the difference between the pre-war and post-war liveries.

Two children lean on the wrought iron rails of the open balcony on this sunny afternoon, oblivious to the impending closure of the tram route and the end of their exhilarating, windy tram rides.

One wonders how many of the 50-plus passengers on the leading tram were looking at the Imperial Cinema (whose canopy is just visible next to the Moseley Road sign on the extreme left of the picture) and considering whether they should go and see Alan Ladd and Robert Preston in the film *Whispering Smith*. The Imperial Picture Palace opened on 26 January 1914 and finally closed in 1983. It was on the night of 25 October 1940 during the showing of an earlier film starring Robert Preston with Dorothy Lamour, somewhat inappropriately titled *Typhoon*, that a bomb dropped through the nearby Carlton Cinema and exploded in front of the screen. Nineteen people were killed and many of them were still sitting upright in their seats, unmarked, but dead. The blast had burst their lungs!

Opposite the cinema is Edward Road, which provided access to the 37 and 39 routes from the depot (see page 76). The area between Edward Road and Balsall Heath Road had been nicknamed 'bomb alley' during the Second World War because of the amount of high explosives dropped on it between autumn 1940 and spring 1941. *R. Brook*

Bottom With the Brighton Road traffic lights on red, car 337, on the 48 route, waits at the head of a queue of cyclists, a Morris 10 and an Austin 16 hp.

This section of Moseley Road had become important, with its baths, library, Friends' Institute, Art School and numerous churches, because it was the centre of the briefly independent Balsall Heath between 1862 and 1891. Prior to its annexation by Birmingham, the council, or Local Board as it was known, built up the infrastructure of the area, much of which remains today.

UEC open-balcony car 337 was only drafted into Moseley Road's allocation of trams from Washwood Heath depot five weeks before the abandonment. It was the last tram to work on the 39 route from Hill Street to Alcester Lanes End via Balsall Heath on 1 October 1949. *R. T. Wilson*

Moseley Road Depot, Kings Heath and Alcester Lanes End

Left Looking southwards along Moseley Road from the Brighton Road traffic lights towards Moseley Road depot, obscured by car 429, we can see the climb towards Park Road where the 39 route from Balsall Heath joined the main route.

Car 429 is working inbound from Kings Heath via Leopold Street to the Hill Street terminus, and is being followed by 435, again working into the city but on the 42 route to Albert Street; the latter car is opposite the entrance to Moseley Road depot. The land behind the trees to the right was used for overnight parking of buses by Birmingham City Transport while the completion of the conversion of the depot to bus operation took place. In the far distance is a Daimler COG5 working towards the city on the 35 route. *R. T. Wilson*

Middle Grey-painted, four-wheel tram 345 stands in the dark recesses of Moseley Road depot early in October 1947 in store and awaiting scrapping, after having been the penultimate tram on the Ladywood 33 route on the night of Saturday 30 August 1947. It would remain in this state until January 1948 when it was finally broken up by George Cohen & Son Ltd. Of the 50 cars of the 301 Class painted in wartime grey, 345 was one of only five not to revert to the standard blue and cream livery.

To the left is car 449, which had been only the third member of the 401 Class to be withdrawn. It would languish even longer in Moseley Road depot before finally being scrapped on 12 November 1949. A massive sort-out of some 25 withdrawn four-wheelers took place between October 1948 and January 1949.

On the extreme left is van 5, which was built at Kyotts Lake Road Works in 1913. It was mounted on a Brill 21E truck and was used for most of its career as a sand van, before being broken up in August 1949. The pre-war-liveried tram behind it appears to be car 566, which was at Moseley Road for electrical re-cabling. The totally enclosed bogie car on the right is car 531, which was also being re-cabled at the depot. *F. N. Lloyd Jones*

Left On Friday 26 August 1949 one of the UEC-built air and oil brake cars, 422, still in its pre-war livery, stands outside the imposing frontage of the depot. Situated just beyond Brighton Road, it two entrances from Moseley Road on either side of the office buildings; a set of tracks can be seen just beneath 422, and the second set in front of car 339. This latter car had been drafted in from Miller Street to cover for a shortage of trams and, despite its post-war livery, was due to be withdrawn when the Moseley Road routes were closed on Saturday 1 October 1949.

Unlike UEC-bodied four-wheeler 339, which had at least 17 changes of depot and operated all over the city, the 401-450 Class spent virtually all their working life at Moseley Road depot; car 422 was one of the final 38 of the class to operate the last narrow-gauge, open-balcony, regular, all-day service in Britain.

Seen between the two trams is the Moseley & Balsall Heath Institute. Built in 1883 and designed in a pseudo-ecclesiastical Gothic style by a local builder, John Bowen, it was to become the cultural focus of the Balsall Heath area. One night in October 1940, when a jazz band was playing at the Institute, a bomb went straight through the roof of the depot next door and straight through one end of car 514. Fortunately the bomb did not go off, otherwise a certain tramway photographer who was the tenor saxophonist that night would not have been able to have taken some of the photographs that appear in this and the companion volumes. *T. J. Edgington*

Top With abandonment approaching, the 401 Class were not all repainted in the post-war livery, and the previous lined-out style with primrose rocker panels became increasingly weatherbeaten. Car 418 climbs Moseley Road at the Park Road junction, where Balsall Heath trams met the main Moseley Road route, on 9 July 1949 when working the Alcester Lanes End service from Albert Street (see also page 77). The passengers on the open balcony get a little protection from the wing window opposite the stair-head, but by 1949 passengers on public transport were expecting something a little better. Despite being fitted with transverse cushioned seats in the lower saloon, these trams belonged to the pre-First World War level of technology. Lack of investment in the tramway system from the mid-1930s gradually introduced the idea among the Transport Committee and Birmingham's public that the trams were an anachronism. Of course, with no new stock after 1930 this became increasingly true and furthered the ever more convincing argument for abandonment.

The new post-war generation of buses, as exemplified by the Leyland Titan PD2/1 bodied by Brush, follows the tram working the 35 bus route to the Maypole terminus. This particular bus is the first of the class, numbered 1656 (HOV 656), and can easily be recognised as, for its first year or so in service, it carried its number-plate on the radiator, before it was moved to the more orthodox cab dash. These buses were splendid vehicles and pointed towards the more comfortable mode of transport that would replace the trams. The new bus services would be numbered 48, 49 and 50, thus replacing the 13 tram services and bus route 35 that plied along Moseley Road. It would, however, be of little comfort to the windswept balcony passengers on tram 418 to know that 1656, in common with all Birmingham's half-cab double-deckers, would not be fitted with heaters! *T. J. Edgington*

Middle On Monday 26 September 1949 car 427 approaches the junction with Park Road as it travels towards the city on the 42 route. It is passing the splendidly styled 1930s petrol pumps, which are selling the present-day well-known brands of Shell and Esso and the long forgotten Cleveland brand. In the background bogie car 728 is waiting at Park Road, which is about half way between Moseley Road depot and Moseley village. Park Road had originally been used by the Balsall Heath steam tram route into the city from 1884 until its abandonment on the last day of 1906 (see page 76). The same route was used by Birmingham Corporation, but when the electric tram route was closed, just five days after this photograph was taken, the replacement bus services did not use Park Road, which resumed its original role as a thoroughfare of lesser important. *A. N. H. Glover*

Bottom Beyond Park Road the tram route negotiated two curves, then fell gently towards Moseley Village. The Prince of Wales public house really marked the start of the shopping area at Moseley, and on a miserable day in 1949 car 445 has just passed the pub and is standing at the last request stop before St Mary's Row in the centre of the late-19th-century suburb. The tram is probably delaying the snub-nosed 1937 Fordson delivery van, while on the left the Coventry-registered Rover Twelve shows that the art of car parking and car abandonment was just as prevalent in 1949 as it is today! *F. N. Lloyd Jones*

Moseley Road depot's allocation of trams had normally been not just the open-balconied four-wheelers of the 401 Class, but also a number of bogie cars. As many as 30 such totally enclosed tramcars had been allocated to the depot before 1939, but the allocation was gradually reduced to none over the next three years. However, from August 1947 the 11 cars of the 702 Class from the sequence 716 to 731 that survived the Second World War returned to Moseley Road.

Car 717, one of these 1925 Brush-built, all-electric bogie cars, leaves St Mary's Row inbound to the city on the 39 route. In early post-war days bogie cars were usually confined to the Balsall Heath service from Hill Street.

The tram is carrying the advertisement for 'Tizer, The Appetizer', a drink that came in a peculiarly erotically shaped bottle. The prospect of purchasing a small bottle of Tizer always seemed to be reaching far more into the realms of the adult world than, say, a bottle of lemonade! *Lens of Sutton*

The steeply gabled Edwardian shops in Moseley village, where car 409 waits at the tram stop before travelling towards the city via Balsall Heath on the 39 route, have barely changed since 1949. This view of car 409 is taken at the same location as that above, but from the other side of the road. The open-balconied tram is passing a large 1938 Walsall-registered Hillman six-cylinder saloon. Before the Second World War Hillman manufactured large luxury cars; this model was later developed as the Humber Snipe.

Overtaking the somewhat down-at-heel tram with its weatherbeaten paintwork is a wartime Austin 30 cwt van. This belonged to a type that ranged from this, the smallest, up to 5-ton lorries and, because they had the general appearance of one of their main competitors, they were known as 'Birmingham Bedfords'. *R. T. Wilson*

Still painted with a dark roof in 1949, a relic from the wartime blackout restrictions, Metro-Cammell-bodied Daimler COG5 single-decker 57, AOP 57, waits for the traffic lights to turn to green before negotiating the junction with Salisbury Road in Moseley village. This 1935-built bus is running empty to take up service in the city, hence the destination display; it had been used throughout the wartime period as an ambulance.

Tram 426 is really working on the 42 route, but the unusual destination number 67 was put up for the benefit of the photographer.

Salisbury Road to the right was cut in the 1890s and was named after the Conservative Prime Minister, the Marquess of Salisbury. He was the Prime Minister three times and died in 1903, just one year after the end of his last seven-year tenure of that office. *W. A. Camwell*

Top It is not often that one can look at a pair of 'before and after' views with a gap of 35 years between them, but have the most recent view dating from 1949!

In the older view we see car 421, one of the 50 UEC-bodied open-balcony cars introduced between August 1912 and March 1913 and fitted with Mountain & Gibson 7 ft 6 in trucks and Dick, Kerr DK19A 40 hp motors. Although earmarked for the new Spencer-Dawson air and oil brake, they were placed in service over the BCT system as the need demanded until the new brakes became available. Being low-height cars, at 15 ft 7½ in, they could pass beneath Aston Station and Selly Oak railway bridges. Once fitted with the air and oil brake, which failed with the brakes locked on, all the class were allocated to Moseley Road depot and were then allowed to work on the 1 in 13 hill in Leopold Street on the 40 and 41 routes (see page 68).

As car 421 is fitted with flop-over boards showing the destination and has the route identification letter 'M', this photograph has to have been taken by 1915, when the letter system fell into disuse. In fact, car 421 is working the steep Leopold Street route where its oil and air brake would be employed.

The tower on the right belongs to the splendid terracotta-detailed Fighting Cocks pub which was built in 1899 at a cost of £4,000 by the Holt Brewery Company along with the shops in St Mary's Row, also to the right; they were built in a vaguely Dutch style, and have a certain architectural panache about them, unlike the steeply gabled shops opposite. *Commercial postcard*

Middle Compared to the 1915 view not a lot has changed in Moseley. Unlike the 401 Class with their Spencer-Dawson air and oil brakes, tram 389 was precluded form working on the Leopold Street route. This tram had been transferred from Coventry Road depot in March 1944 and stayed at Moseley Road until it was withdrawn for scrap on 1 October 1949. It belonged to the repeat order of UEC cars numbered in the 361-400 series, placed in late 1911, which were 12 inches longer than the previous 60 trams; this was so that the platform could accommodate a slightly easier staircase.

The tram is carrying an advertisement for the *Evening Despatch* on its balcony dash panels. This local newspaper was printed from 1902 until 1963, when it was absorbed into the *Birmingham Evening Mail*. Along the side of the tram is an advertisement for the Co-operative group of shops, from which, at the end of each half year, customers could claim back a dividend. *F. N. Lloyd Jones*

Bottom The first member of the UEC-built four-wheelers of 1913, car 401, leaves the Reddings Road stop when working the 42 route in the summer of 1949. The tram will go down the hill and past the police station on its way to Moseley Village some quarter of a mile away. This tram stop not only served the large houses in the area, but also the Moseley Rugby Football Club, the premier rugby side in Birmingham, whose ground, The Reddings, is situated in Reddings Road. *R. T. Wilson*

Below Once out of Moseley, Alcester Road climbed a steady gradient known as Welsh's Hill and passed the entrance to Moseley Hall. This Georgian house was built by the Taylors, a banking family who formed a partnership that is still with us today in the form of Lloyds Bank. The hall

was burned down in 1791 when anti-Republican fervour amongst a Tory-inspired drunken mob resulted in the so-called 'Church and King Riots' in which anyone with Republican sympathies was attacked. The hall was rebuilt in 1796, but by 1884 had been purchased by Richard Cadbury, the chocolate manufacturer. Two years later the Cadburys moved to Uffculme House in Moor Green and gave Moseley Hall to Birmingham as a gift for use as a convalescent home.

Once over the hill at Moor Green Lane, Alcester Road drops down to the junction with Queensbridge Road, where four-wheel car 438 is seen on 19 April 1947. It is travelling away from Moseley village and would have passed Moseley Hall about two minutes earlier. The tram has just passed the junction across which a young, short-trousered cyclist pedals carefully over the tram tracks. *T. J. Edgington*

Below left Just beyond Queensbridge Road is the bridge that carries the High Street over the former Birmingham & Gloucester Railway, opened in 1840. It runs in a cutting behind the advertising hoardings just above the Austin Ten that is turning into Valentine Road. A rather full tramcar, 420 is working on the 39 route to Alcester Lanes End via Balsall Heath in April 1947, and is about to stop opposite the entrance to Kings Heath Station, although the tram is six years too late to link up with the trains, the station having closed on 27 January 1941!

Birmingham Corporation's advertising policy, with hindsight, regularly produced a peculiar juxtaposition of advertisements. Car 420 is carrying the 'Drink delicious Typhoo Tea, so very refreshing!' advertisement, but the obsession with laxatives such as Ex-Lax and Beechams Pills may suggest that people's concern with their digestive tracts is less today than then. *A. N. H. Glover collection*

Bottom The village of Kings Heath, known as Kyngesheth in 1511, grew in a linear pattern in the mid-19th century along what was later to become known as High Street. It first became a separate parish on 13 January 1863, and was still part of Kings Norton UDC when the steam tram route was extended from Moseley Village to the terminus at Institute Road on 1 February 1887.

The High Street later became a major suburban shopping centre as can be seen from the 1920s shops next to the tram, including a branch of the well-known grocery chain of George Mason.

The Kings Heath and Moseley Institute, whose church-like tower can be seen behind the tram, was built in 1878, using money philanthropically donated by J. H. Nettlefold, whose family was part of the Guest, Keen & Nettlefold screw manufacturing company (later known as GKN).

Car 725, which has just passed Institute Road, was one of the 30 cars built in 1925 by Brush. It was placed on EMB Burnley-type maximum traction bogies and had GEC WT32H 40 hp motors. In their final years these bogie cars usually worked on the Cannon Hill and Alcester Lanes End services that went via Balsall Heath; here, in 1949, car 725 is working such a route, the 39 service, and is being followed by car 423 working the 42 route. Members of the 702 Class spent most of their working lives before and after the Second World War operating from Moseley Road, but their brief sojourn at Miller Street and Witton in the early part of the war saw no fewer than nine of them destroyed at the latter depot. One more tram was destroyed in Miller Street in April 1941 and a further car was withdrawn as an accident victim. In addition to these, a further 11 trams, including 725, received some structural damage. *F. N. Lloyd Jones*

Top At the far end of the shopping centre of Kings Heath the spire of All Saints Church dominates the skyline. When this photograph was taken it was only some 15 years since it had been completed with the building of its south-west tower.

Car 88, with flop-over destination boards and displaying the route letter 'M', stands at the top of High Street in about 1910. It was one of the Mountain & Gibson 8 ft 6 in Radial truck cars built by UEC between August 1906 and March 1907. They were originally open-balcony and open-vestibule trams, but all had their vestibules enclosed from 1923. These 52-seater trams were quite tall at 16 ft 0½ in, but could negotiate the Stratford Road and Coventry Road railway bridges. Car 88 would be replaced on the Moseley Road services by 1914 when the 401 Class took over the running of most of the services.

The radial trucks under these trams were a source of trouble within a few months of entering service; in practice this meant that after the tram turned a corner the axle on the truck did not return to the straight position. In an attempt to cure the problem the trucks were made rigid, but the alteration was not a complete success. After 19 years of alterations and replacements, all the remaining radial trucks were replaced on the 71 Class, with no fewer than 135 of the class, including car 88, being placed on Peckham P35 trucks. *Commercial postcard*

Middle The wall to the right of tramcar 416 on this photograph, taken on Friday 2 September 1949, belongs to All Saints Church. Identical car 425, incidentally repainted in post-war livery with the simpler style of post-war fleet number, is working on the 40 short-working to Kings Heath, and will take the cross-over to stand behind 416, which has also worked to this destination, but which will return to Hill Street via Leopold Street.

The view out of the city looking south-westwards has changed out of all recognition today. Car 425 is opposite the subterranean public lavatories that stood in the middle of Vicarage Road, which were finally replaced in 1993. Also having disappeared over the intervening years are all the distant trees in the main Alcester Road South beyond All Saints Road, which were cut down in the 1960s when an anonymous low-height concrete box structure of shops was built. Today the site of these shops is mainly occupied by a Sainsbury's supermarket. *T. J. Edgington*

Bottom Beyond Kings Heath the trams ran down to the Howard Road crossing before climbing a long gentle gradient to the Alcester Lanes End terminus. Here car 414, working the 42 route, approaches the junction from the Kings Heath direction early in 1949.

Although the small terrace of houses has been demolished, this stretch of Alcester Road South is still recognisably the same; this is despite numerous plans to upgrade the road since the nearby M40/M42 was opened, which made parts of Birmingham including Kings Heath more accessible to car-borne commuters. *F. N. Lloyd Jones*

Left The last day of the Kings Heath tram routes was Saturday 1 October 1949. A normal service was maintained throughout the day and the trams were used, as they had been for many years, to provide the service for that evening's Kings Heath dog-track meeting at the racecourse just beyond the tram terminus. This line-up of trams, seen at about six o'clock that evening, is standing near the terminus, just north of the junction with Taylor Road, and is led by car 731; this was the last all-electric bogie car to enter service with Birmingham Corporation, some 24 years earlier. The intending spectators, leaving the trams for the last time, would have the option of brand new Daimler CVD6 buses on the service for the next meeting. Unusually, car 731 has worked the 42 route from Albert Street rather than the more normal 401 Class four-wheelers which are lined up behind it. In the distance is one of the 1948 batch of Leyland Titan PD2/1s, which, like 731, had Brush bodies. Kings Heath dog track closed in March 1971 and its site is now a housing estate. *A. N. H. Glover*

Right On the last day of operation, 1 October 1949, and looking in need of the repaint that it would never receive, car 447 stands at the same location near Taylor Road, where the 18 bus crossed Alcester Road South.

Carrying the balcony dash advertisement for the Kings Heath ladies outfitter, E. R. Green, this tram, in company with the rest of the 401 Class that had survived to the end of tramcar operation, would later be driven back to Moseley Road depot where it would be broken up by George Cohen & Sons Ltd as one of the final nine cars of the class to be scrapped in December 1949.

These open-balcony cars ran on average some 858,000 miles in their 37 years' service. One wonders if a 1957-built double-decker bus would be welcomed as anything other than a museum piece if it turned up today on an all-day working on the Alcester Road routes. *A. N. H. Glover*

Left On Thursday 14 April 1939, the same day that Adolf Hitler drove into Vienna, Brush totally enclosed car 714 stands at the Alcester Lanes End terminus, Kings Heath, preparing to work back to Hill Street via Balsall Heath. The driver is passing a few moments with his conductor before clocking in at the Bundy clock, which is just behind the bread van.

This tram was unfortunate as it became the first bogie car to be taken out of service. It overturned, after a combination of a faulty controller and failure by the motorman to obey braking regulations, at the bottom of the long hill on the corner of Park Road and Witton Lane in March 1940. The top deck was badly damaged and after being stored throughout the war in Sampson Road paint shop it was broken up by August 1945. *H. B. Priestley*

BIRMINGHAM TRAMS 1933-53

Right At 11.05 am on Sunday 23 January 1949, car 407 waits for further passengers at the Alcester Lanes End terminus. It is standing outside the Kings Arms public house before taking the main Moseley Road route into the city centre. Exactly one month later, on 24 February, car 407 was repainted, presumably at considerable expense, in the post-war livery and with plain fleet numbers, despite being scheduled for withdrawal in October 1948!

Because of the Second World War, these trams remained in service well beyond their expected lifespan. However, they did have the advantage of having the air and oil brake, which allowed them to run over all Moseley Road depot's routes. As long as there were insufficient bogie cars and the Moseley Road group of services were being kept running, the 401 Class was safe. Nine months later the routes had closed, the 401s were being broken up by George Cohen & Sons in the depot, which had been their home for 37 years, and all the totally enclosed allocation of 702 Class bogie cars had been transferred to Miller Street.

The side window destination blind for this route reads ALCESTER LANES END AND DALE END, when in fact the terminus was in Albert Street; Dale End had been used from 1921 to 1930, when the central island in this wide street had on it an elaborately decorated cast-iron, glass-roofed shelter. The Alcester Lanes End trams, together with those that traversed Coventry Road, Stratford Road and Warwick Road, all terminated there; however, although the 42, 48, 50 and 65 routes moved into Albert Street, some trams still retained this rather confusing destination display as their linen blinds were virtually indestructible. *A. N. H. Glover*

Middle The scene at the Kings Arms in August 1993 had altered remarkably little. The mode of transport had changed in the intervening years to a 73-seater MCW 'Metrobus' II, in this case 2903 (C903 FON), owned by the privatised West Midlands Travel, which competes on the Moseley Road routes with at least three other bus operators.

The Kings Arms is still a rather unconvincing mock-Elizabethan building, although its function has changed from just a public house to a steak house. Similarly, the owners of the shops have long since gone and the trade of their former premises has changed, but the fabric of the shops, down as far as the distant Woodthorpe Road junction, has remained largely unaltered. *D. R. Harvey*

Right Looking remarkably spick-and-span, UEC-built car 428 stands at the Alcester Lanes End terminus. The tram is equipped with white-painted fenders and has its headlight masked. Above the tramcar, underneath the bracket arm, is a trolley-finder; these were used during the war at places such as termini where trolleypoles would have to be turned, helping the conductor to guide the pole to the wire and avoid any flashes in the blackout conditions.

Southwards away from the city was Kings Heath dog track, which remained open throughout the hostilities. Beyond that, Alcester Road South had begun to be developed as far as the city boundary at the Maypole, with the inter-war semi-detached houses being separated from the road by the provision of wide grass verges. The meandering, single-carriageway road is still waiting, some 60 years later, for this congested main route to be made into a straighter dual-carriageway, although this may now never happen. *R. T. Wilson*

BIRMINGHAM CITY TRANSPORT ROUTE NUMBERS

The numbering of Birmingham's tram services did not take place until 1915 when it replaced the lettering system that had been adopted in 1907, and which continued the practice that had first been seen on the CBT steam trams. The routes were numbered 1-91 but were not in any chronological or recognisably geographical order; those introduced after 1915 were just given the next vacant number. Many of the numbers were short-workings or depot journeys and this led to a lot of these associated short routes apparently having no numerical connection to the main route.

1 Steelhouse Lane to Stockland Green. Short-working of 78 route 23.6.26. Abandoned 4.7.53. Incorporated into replacement 65 bus route.

20 Steelhouse Lane to Erdington (Chester Road) 24.4.1907. Diverted from High Street, Erdington, 25.9.38 to Sutton New Road. Abandoned 4.7.53. Replaced by 64 bus service.

3 Martineau Street to Witton via Six Ways, Aston. Ex-CBT service. To BCT 1.1.12. Weekdays only after 18.1.31. Abandoned 11.9.39.

3X Martineau Street to Witton via Aston Cross. Ex-CBT service. To BCT 1.1.12. Cut back to Witton Square 9.3.41. Abandoned 31.12.49. Replaced by 39 bus service.

4 Station Street to Stoney Lane (Esme Road). City terminus to Hill Street 1914. Abandoned 5.1.37. Incorporated into replacement 13A bus service.

5 Villa Road, Lozells and Gravelly Hill. Ex-CBT service. To BCT 1.1.12. Abandoned 30.9.50. Replaced by 40A bus service.

6 Martineau Street to Perry Barr (Perry Barr railway station). Abandoned 21.12.49. Incorporated into existing 33 bus service.

7 Martineau Street to Nechells. Outward route via Long Acre, inward via Nechells Park Road. Cut back to Nechells trolleybus service from Old Square.

8 Martineau Street to Alum Rock (Highfield Road). Extended to Belchers Lane (Pelham)

14.10.25. Abandoned 30.9.50. Incorporated into replacement 55 bus service.

9 Martineau Street to Ward End (Sladefield Road). Short-working of 10 route.

10 Martineau Street to Washwood Heath (Fox & Goose). Abandoned 30.9.1950. Incorporated into replacement 56 bus service.

11 High Street to Bordesley Green (Blake Lane) via Fazeley Street. Short-working of 90 service 31.10.28. Abandoned 2.10.48. Replaced by 51 bus service.

12 High Street to Bordesley Green (Blake Lane) via Deritend and Coventry Road. Extended to Eastfield Road, Bordesley Green East 4.11.25. Short-working of 84 service 26.8.28. Abandoned 2.10.48. Replaced by 52 bus service.

13 High Street to Small Heath Park. Formerly part of cross-city service to Nechells. Short-working of 15 service. Abandoned 6.1.34. Incorporated into 92 trolleybus service.

14 Station Street to Small Heath Park. Short-working of 16 service after 1.1.12. Abandoned 6.1.34. Incorporated into 93 trolleybus service.

15 High Street to Church Road, Yardley. Abandoned 6.1.34. Replaced by 92 trolleybus route.

16 Station Street to Church Road, Yardley. Originally CBT service. Joint CBT/BCT service 1.1.07. Entirely to BCT 1.1.12. Abandoned 6.1.34. Replaced by 93 trolleybus service.

17 High Street to Stratford Road (College Road). Extended to Fox Hollies Road/Highfield Road 31.5.14. Extended to Hall Green (Shirley Boundary) 2.4.28. Abandoned 5.1.37. Replaced by 37 bus service.

18 Station Street to Stratford Road (College Road). Extended to Fox Hollies Road (Shirley Boundary) 2.4.28. Abandoned 5.1.37. Replaced by 46 bus service.

19 High Street to Stratford Road (St John's Road). Short-working of 17 service. Abandoned 5.1.37. Incorporated into replacement 37 and 38 bus services.

20 Station Street to Stratford Road (St John's Road). Incorporated into replacement 46 and 47 bus services.

21 Station Street to Stratford Road (College Road). Short-working of 18 route.

Abandoned 5.1.37. Incorporated into replacement 46 bus service.

22 Station Street to Bolton Road (Waverley Road). Abandoned 4.2.30. Replaced by 22 bus service.

23 Colmore Row to The Hawthorns, Handsworth. Abandoned 1.4.39. Replaced by 72 bus service.

24 Colmore Row to Lozells via Wheeler Street and Hamstead Road (anti-clockwise with 25 route). Cut back to Villa Cross 7.8.33. Abandoned 1.4.39. Replaced by 69 bus service.

25 Colmore Row to Lozells via Hamstead Road and Wheeler Street (clockwise with 24 route). Abandoned 7.8.33.

26 Colmore Row to Oxhill Road via Soho Road and Grove Lane. Abandoned 1.4.39. Replaced by 70 bus service.

27 Colmore Row to Stafford Road, Soho Road, Handsworth. Short-working of 26 route. Abandoned 1.4.39.

28 Colmore Row to New Inns, Crocketts Lane, Handsworth. Short-working of 23 route. Abandoned 1.4.39. Replaced by 71 bus service.

29 Edmund Street to Bearwood. Joint service with Birmingham & Midland 1.4.28. Abandoned 30.9.39. Replaced by B82 bus service.

30 Edmund Street to Windmill Lane, Cape Hill, Smethwick. Joint service with Birmingham & Midland 1.7.06 as short-working of 29 route but operated entirely by BCT. Abandoned 30.9.39. Replaced by B81 bus service.

31 Edmund Street to Soho Station. Joint service with Birmingham & Midland 1.7.06 but operated entirely by BCT. Abandoned 30.9.39. Replaced by B83 bus service.

32 Edmund Street to Lodge Road (Foundry Road). Abandoned 29.3.47. Replaced by 96 bus service.

33 Navigation Street to Ladywood (Icknield Port Road). Abandoned 30.8.47. Replaced by 95 bus service.

34 Navigation Street to Hagley Road. (1st Class service 15.2.14-19.5.14.) Abandoned 9.8.30. Replaced by 34 bus service.

35 Navigation Street to Selly Oak. Ex-CBT service. Taken over by BCT 1.7.11. Short-working of 69 route after 1.10.23. Abandoned 5.7.52. Incorporated into replacement 62 and 63 bus services.

36 Navigation Street to Selly Oak. Ex-CBT service. Taken over by BCT 1.7.11. Abandoned 5.7.52. Incorporated into replacement 45 bus service.

37 Navigation Street to Cannon Hill (Willows Road). Abandoned 1.10.49. Replaced by extended 48 bus service.

38 Hill Street to High Street/Vicarage Road, Kings Heath, via Balsall Heath. Short-working of 39 service. Abandoned 1.10.49. Incorporated into replacement 48 bus service.

39 Hill Street to Alcester Lanes End via Balsall Heath. Abandoned 1.10.49. Replaced by extended 48 bus service.

40 Hill Street to High Street/Vicarage Road, Kings Heath, via Leopold Street. Short-working of 51 route. Abandoned 1.10.49. Replaced by 49 bus service.

41 Navigation Street to Moseley Road/Trafalgar Road (Moseley Road depot). Short-working of 40 route. Abandoned 1.10.49. Incorporated into replacement 49B bus service.

42 High Street to Alcester Lanes End via Bradford Street and Moseley Road. Abandoned 1.10.49. Incorporated into replacement 50 bus service.

43 High Street to Station Road, Kings Heath, via Bradford Street and Moseley Road. Short-working of 42 route. Absorbed into other services after about 1923.

44 High Street to Acocks Green (Broad Road) via Warwick Road 2.2.16. Extended to Acocks Green centre (Shirley Road) 9.10.1922. Abandoned 5.1.37. Replaced by 44 bus service.

45 High Street to Walford Road, Sparkbrook 2.2.16. Abandoned 5.1.37. Incorporated into replacement 37 bus service.

46 Navigation Street to Stirchley (British Oak) 1919. Short-working of 36 route. Abandoned 5.7.52. Incorporated into replacement 45 bus service.

47 Hill Street to Station Road, Kings Heath, via Leopold Street 1919. Absorbed into other services after about 1923.

48 High Street to High Street/Vicarage Road, Kings Heath. Short-working of 42 route. Abandoned 1.10.49. Incorporated into replacement 50 bus service.

49 Navigation Street to Mary Street/Park Road, Balsall Heath. Short-working of 39 route. Abandoned 1.10.49. Incorporated into replacement 48 bus route.

50 High Street to Moseley Road/Trafalgar Road (Moseley Road depot). Abandoned 1.10.49. Absorbed into replacement 50 bus service.

51 Hill Street to Alcester Lanes End via Leopold Street. Abandoned 1.10.49.

52 Hill Street to Station Road, Kings Heath, via Balsall Heath about 1919. Short-working of 39 service. Absorbed into other services after about 1923.

53 Navigation Street to Dogpool Lane, Pershore Road, about 1919. Incorporated into replacement 45 bus service.

54 Priory Road/Pebble Mill Road short-working of 35 service about 1919. Abandoned 5.7.52. Incorporated into replacement 62 and 63 bus services.

55 Edmund Street to Dudley Road/Grove Lane (city boundary). Short-working of 29 service. Abandoned 30.9.39. Replaced by B80 bus service.

56 High Street to Hay Mills ?.2.19. Short-working of 15 service. Abandoned 6.1.34. Replaced by 56 trolleybus service.

57 Station Street to Hay Mills ?.2.19. Short-working of 16 service. Abandoned 6.1.34. Replaced by 57 trolleybus service.

58 High Street to Stoney Lane/Stratford Road about 1917. Short-working of 19 service. Not used after about 1920.

59 Steelhouse Lane to Gravelly Hill about 1920. Short-working of 1 and 2 services. Abandoned 4.7.53. Incorporated into replacement 64, 65 and 66 bus services.

60 Steelhouse Lane to Aston Cross about 1920. Short-working of 1 and 2 services. Abandoned 4.7.53. Incorporated into replacement 64, 65 and 66 bus services.

61 Martineau Street to Gate Inn, Saltley, about 1920. Short-working of 8, 9 and 10 services. Abandoned 30.9.50. Incorporated into replacement 55 and 56 bus services.

62 Washwood Heath to Great Francis Street about 1920. Inward working of 10 service. Abandoned 30.9.50. Incorporated into replacement 56 bus service.

63 Steelhouse Lane to Holly Lane/Tyburn Road 13.5.20. Short-working of 79 service 20.7.27-12.2.30. Extended into Holly Lane to Fort Dunlop 13.2.30. Abandoned 4.7.53.

64 Steelhouse Lane to High Street, Erdington, about 1920. Short-working of 2 service. Diverted to Barnabas Road/Sutton New Road 25.9.38. Abandoned 4.7.53. Incorporated into replacement 64 bus service.

65 Hill Street to Moseley via Leopold Street about 1920. Short-working of 40 and 51 services. Abandoned 1.10.49. Incorporated into replacement 49 service.

66 Hill Street to Moseley via Balsall Heath about 1920. Short-working of 38 and 39 services. Abandoned 1.1.0.49. Incorporated into 48 bus service.

67 Dale End to Moseley via Bradford Street about 1920. Short-working of 42 and 48 services. Abandoned 1.10.49. Incorporated into replacement 50 bus service.

68 Villa Road to Soho Road, Lozells, Gravelly Hill and Erdington (Chester Road) about 1920 as Sundays-only service. Abandoned without replacement 1923.

69 Navigation Street to Northfield (The Bell) 1.10.23 as extension of 35 route. Abandoned 5.7.52. Incorporated into replacement 62 and 63 bus service.

70 Navigation Street to Rednal 14.4.24. Abandoned 5.7.52. Replaced by 62 bus service.

71 Navigation Street to Rubery (Cock Hill Lane) 8.2.26. Abandoned 5.7.52. Replaced by 63 bus service.

72 Navigation Street to Longbridge 17.12.23. Short-working of 70 route after 14.4.24. Abandoned 5.7.52. Incorporated into replacement 62 and 63 bus service.

73 Livery Street to Carters Green, West Bromwich, 1.4.24. Short-working of 74 and 75 services. Abandoned 1.4.39. Replaced by 73 bus service.

74 Livery Street to Dudley (Tipton Road) via West Bromwich. Ex-South Staffordshire (lessee 1.7.11-31.3.24). Taken over by BCT 1.4.24. Abandoned 1.4.39. Replaced by 74 bus service.

75 Livery Street to Wednesbury (White Horse). Part of South Staffordshire (lessee) service. Taken over by BCT 1.4.24. Abandoned 1.4.39. Replaced by 75 bus route.

76 Colmore Row to Great Bridge 1925. Short-working of 74 service. Abandoned 1.4.39. Replaced by 76 bus service.

77 Colmore Row to Spon Lane/High Street, West Bromwich, 1925. Short-working of 73, 74, 75 and 76 services. Replaced by 77 bus service.

78 Steelhouse Lane to Short Heath 23.6.26. Abandoned 4.7.53. Replaced by 65 bus route.

79 Steelhouse Lane to Pype Hayes Park 20.7.27. Abandoned 4.7.53. Replaced by 66 bus route.

80 Edmund Street to St Paul's Road, Smethwick. Ex-Birmingham & Midland. Short-working of 87 service. Taken over by BCT 1.4.28. Abandoned 30.9.39. Replaced by B84 bus service.

81 Villa Road to Soho Road, Lozells to Pype Hayes summer 1928 as Sundays-only service. Abandoned without replacement 1930.

82 High Street to Stratford Road (Fox Hollies Road/Highfield Road) 2.4.28. Short-working of 17 route. Abandoned 5.1.37. Replaced by 38 bus service.

83 Station Street to Stratford Road (Fox Hollies Road/Highfield Road) 2.4.28. Short-working of 18 route. Abandoned 5.1.37. Replaced by 46 bus service.

84 Albert Street to Stechford (Stuarts Road) via Deritend and Coventry Road 26.8.28. Abandoned 2.10.48. Replaced by 54 bus route.

85 Edmund Street to Spon Lane, West Bromwich, via Smethwick. Ex-Birmingham & Midland. Short-working of 87 service. Taken over by BCT 1.4.28. Abandoned 30.9.39. Replaced by B85 bus service.

86 Edmund Street to Oldbury via Smethwick. Ex-Birmingham & Midland. Short-working of 87 service. Taken over by BCT 1.4.28. Abandoned 30.9.39. Replaced by B86 service.

87 Edmund Street to Dudley (Tipton Road) via Smethwick and Oldbury. Ex-Birmingham & Midland. Taken over by BCT 1.4.28. Abandoned 30.9.39. Replaced by B87 bus service.

88 Windmill Lane to Spon Lane, West Bromwich, via Smethwick. Ex-Birmingham & Midland. Taken over by BCT 1.4.28. Short-working of 87 service. Abandoned 30.9.39. Replaced by B88 bus route.

89 High Street to Stratford Road (College Road) 2.4.28. Short-working of 17 route. Abandoned 5.1.37. Incorporated into replacement 38 bus service.

90 Albert Street to Stechford (Stuarts Road) via Fazeley Street 31.10.28. Abandoned 2.10.48. Replaced by 53 bus service.

91 High Street to Warwick Road, Tyseley (Stockfield Road) 1929. Short-working of 44 route. Abandoned 5.1.37. Incorporated into replacement 44 bus service.

INDEX OF STREET NAMES AND TRAM ROUTES

Figures in (brackets) are route numbers. Words in CAPITALS are terminal points and areas of Birmingham.